10.95

CRAZY WOMEN IN THE RAFTERS

CRAZY WOMEN IN THE RAFTERS

MEMORIES OF A TEXAS BOYHOOD

BY

PAUL PATTERSON

NORMAN : UNIVERSITY OF OKLAHOMA PRESS

Library of Congress Cataloging in Publication Data
Patterson, Paul, 1909–
    Crazy women in the rafters.
    1. Patterson, Paul, 1909–   I. Title.
CT275.P453A33   976.4'06'0924 [B]   74-34035
ISBN 0-8061-1280-8

To the memory of Papa and Mama, whose combined attendance in the School of Hard Knocks totaled some 189 years with no absences, few tardies, and still fewer whimperings or complaints.

PREFACE

Until confronted with documented proof to the contrary I hereby lay claim to the covered-wagon-moving-championship of the world. Not in distance, perhaps, but in numbers—*thirty-six* moves. I claim this title for myself alone, since all other Pattersons have been trying, lo these fifty years, to forget it.

Even if challenged I will not subtract a single number from that three dozen, but I could take the wagon sheet off for a half dozen or so, these moves being in good weather and for short distances. These thirty-six moves, ranging in distances of two hundred miles (Roscoe to Balmorhea) down to two hundred yards (Upland jail apartment to Upland phone office) are counting only from Papa's and Mama's marriage in 1900 until our last move as a family unit in 1924. Moves thereafter do not count, as they were by motor vehicle.

We kids used to speculate upon what Papa's life would have been like if he hadn't married and settled down. Likely he would have turned out just another *drifting cowboy*. In fact, that is what Mama decided he still was. Or that he had gotten into a (covered wagon) rut, to say the least. Consequently, after *twenty-nine* she quit us, hoping to take permanent root somewhere.

Not that Papa was restless, shiftless, useless, or irresponsible.

Itinerant perhaps, yes, resulting from a situation so complicated, so complex that it will take at least 270 pages to explain.

In later years Mama wound up with as strong a case of the go-yonders as Papa ever had, so why didn't they make it as a team? Destiny. Fate, pure and simple. The cards never seemed to fall right; the stars were never in the right places at the right times, "adverse planetary aspects" say the astrologers. Their widely divergent make-ups produced the first strike against them. The only thing they had in common was a wagonful of kids. Well, there were a couple of other qualities they shared in common: unlimited optimism and a boundless faith in every human creature—except each other. Fact is, this unbounded faith in humanity was the very seat of their trouble. In any deal, contract, or transaction their gullibility exceeded their ability. Papa, for example, knew the horse from forelock to fetlock, from cannon to coronet, but he didn't know horse traders. Consequently, he was nearly always *nearly* afoot in a land where the horse was an absolute necessity.

Mama, in the world of commerce, fared just as poorly. Once when she felt that she had accumulated an excess of household wares (one item to be exact) she ran the following ad in the Upton County Roundup: Household item in excellent condition to sell or *give away*.

We kids inherited assorted tempers and temperaments from both sides of the wagon. Practical realists for the most part, except in my case—a dreamer of idle dreams and a fabricator of phantoms and fantasies. Yet we all shared that quality common to both Papa and Mama—imperishable optimism. True we fell into gloomy moods, sank into the melancholy poet's "slough of despond," but never into one so deep but what the mere fluttering by of a butterfly wouldn't distract and extract us therefrom. Nor was there ever a gloom so dark that a new pair of shoes, a fairly snug, comparatively dry place to camp, or a single trinket for Christmas would not dispel. In sum, *how* we acted and reacted to adversity was always the same. But *where* was something else, hence this book.

I, Paul Patterson, the sixth child, do hereby maintain that to the best of my knowledge and recollection *Crazy Women in the Rafters* is a true and accurate account—or itinerary, if you will— of the J. D. Patterson family. More than sixty years have rolled by, so maybe *Crazy Women in the Rafters* isn't *exactly* the way it happened in every case. Maybe there wasn't a crazy woman in every nester's abandoned attic. Or maybe there wasn't an almost headless wild man running over in the Y beef pasture. But they were in my mind, right where my big brothers planted them, hence just as terrifying. So what if Pancho Villa didn't show up that night, I couldn't have been scared any worse. And suppose the mule didn't come *that* close to carrying me off a sixty-foot bluff (which might not have been but fifty). And suppose the bootlegger didn't fire but one shot over my head, or maybe no shots, my terror was already beyond the point of no return.

The important thing is that despite poverty, privation—and considerable migration—Papa never expected, nor accepted one cent of charity. And we not only survived but thrived.

Paul Patterson

Crane, Texas
January, 1976

CONTENTS

CRAZY WOMEN IN THE RAFTERS

CHAPTER I

"Moved, oh, Moved to a Different Place" was the title of a song Mama was moved to compose but never seemed to muster the strength or the spirit to sing. Our old Rock Island wagon with its tattered canvas bonnet, wash-tub earrings, and stovepipe necklace was met and/or passed on more West Texas roads than that of the crockery peddler, but without the profitable returns. From Stiles proper (if one can call a half dugout proper) to the Kircheville Ranch north of Stiles to the Bates place out Big Lake to Salt Well below Rankin to Rankin proper to the K. C. M. & O. section house east of Rankin to the Doc Johnson place south of Rankin to the Powell place west of Rankin to the John R. Johnston place southwest of old Upland to the Taylor place east of Upland and so on and on.

Since Papa wasn't a man to live one cent beyond his means, this wagon wanderlust made for some powerful mean living, especially after he lost his job as state cattle inspector back in 1913. A fast-talking cowman with a slow-moving herd had convinced Inspector Patterson that his herd was poor from poverty of pasture not from fever ticks. "Friend," the cowman said "unless this herd can move onto grass, you've taken onto yourself blame for the damnedest die-up since '86. Amongst which will be my wife and little children, apt as not."

Consequently the herd moved on west, uninspected, across the quarantine line. Ex-inspector Patterson was shortly to follow in its wake riding point, flank, and drag on a herd of his own, namely, a sickly wife and five of his seven kids. This herd was not on the verge of a die-up yet, but hunger was never more than a picket rope's length away. And thereafter it was touch and go—mostly go—what with eight moves within the next couple of years. Twenty-four moves, all told, based on Mama's carefully kept tally, with more to come—many more.

Yet the terms vagabond, vagrant, drifter, ne'er-do-well, would have been completely inaccurate, not to say grossly unfair as regards Papa, faltering finances and frequent moves notwithstanding. Papa was not haunted by far horizons, nor was he searching for the pot of gold at the end of the rainbow—just a pot of *frijoles* (for nine) at the end of the day. Nor was Papa shiftless, irresponsible, unreliable, or unskilled. Far from it. He was a good cowhand, a fair-to-middling carpenter, a skilled fence builder, an experienced freighter, and so on. Furthermore, no job was too rugged or too menial as long as it was honest work. In fact, in the first settlement we passed through that qualified as a city Papa had applied for the job of city scavenger. (This was before the sting of it had been softened by the title "sanitary engineer.") Papa's philosophy was that a man desperate for work was more apt to land something aiming too low instead of too high as is generally the case with job hunters. But in either case Papa's aims were futile so far.

There wasn't any outfit anywhere who could say Papa hadn't made them a top hand. Why then so many jobs of so few days and so full of uncertainty? Providence partly but mostly poor bargaining ability on Papa's part. Except for cowboy jobs—scarce as hens' teeth for a family of seven—Papa's work came through contracting mostly, and on these contracts he invariably underbid himself. Some said it was a lack of savvy, a shortage of smart. Not so. It was simply a case of too soft a heart in too hard a time. This plus an ever-pressing financial urgency—bordering on emergency—

which didn't allow a broad enough bargaining base and didn't afford room to maneuver. And, strange as it may sound, too much discipline. Dickering on a deal, Papa always kept us kids back out of sight whereas the party of the other part was invariably encompassed round about by a passel of pitiful young'uns, eyes watering and noses running—something to play, or rather work, on Papa's sympathetic nerve.

"Well, then, I'll fence it for $7 a mile," Papa would say, his eyes beginning to water for the watery-eyed kids. What he was forgetting was that right behind him was a wagonful of his own whose eyes were outwatering and whose noses were outrunning anybody's in the crowd. And what's more, the mere sight of them would have prompted the party of the other part to raise Papa's bid to $14.

CHAPTER II

As a consequence of Papa's losing the cattle inspector's job we wound up in Upland, Texas, county seat of Upton County, our cash in hand totaling seventy-five cents, which went immediately for six bits worth of grub at John R. Johnston's General Mercantile. Other assets—consisting, chiefly, of a team of sway-backed horses with wagon to match—Papa put to immediate use freighting "staple and fancy" groceries up from the new railroad town of Rankin ten miles to the south. Some days the trip would net fifty cents, other days as much as $1.50. Papa, of course, spurned the cash and accepted his pay in groceries. And much to our dismay, when we kids were starved for the "fancies," he accepted only the "staples." What's more, Papa had soon established a good credit—good, we kids surmised, because he wouldn't use it. Consequently, from our point of view, this made living within our means meaner still.

But for a change, and a wonder, we wound up in living quarters to exceed our wildest dreams—a four-room ranch house complete with front and back gallery. Mama was elated. Maybe this move would be the last. Maybe she was unloading those scarred and scanty household furnishings for the last time. (Little did she realize that she was, as we shall see in due course.) At least she had prayed and perhaps had sung that this would be their last move.

6

Our old furniture, if given the power of reasoning and speech, would have added a fervent "amen." It was on its last legs and not just figuratively. For example, that very first morning, with breakfast half cooked, the cookstove fell apart, scattering mesquite embers and baking powder biscuits and splattering flour gravy and sugar molasses far and wide.

Papa, ever resourceful in emergencies, grabbed up the teakettle and quenched the coals in a twinkling. What's more he had the stove back up and breakfast back on to cook before you could say "Jack Roberson." But there wasn't anybody there to eat it. Mama, panic prone to start with, was doubly jooberous of fires, and for good reason; she had already been burned out twice. Before the last biscuit had quit rolling, she had us kids rounded up and a hundred yards out in the black brush. And there we would stay until she was doubly sure the last ember had been quenched.

On top of this Blanche didn't want to be late to school her very first day. Consequently Papa had to hook up the team and get her over there *pronto*. En route, Blanche pointed out another arrow of dust stirred up by another buggy topped with bright, bobbing bonnets and big hats. "I reckon their stove musta fell too," Papa philosophized. It took more than a falling cookstove to ruffle the even tenor of Papa's ways.

The Taylor place was remote enough to be considered a ranch and yet easily accessible to that great and glittering city of Upland a couple of miles to the west. Although I was crowding four years, up to now the earth was without form and void, with only shreds and patches of my eight previous homes projected on occasions before my mind's eye. But here at the Taylor place I was becoming aware of a state of being—of flora and fauna, if black brush (which we called greasewood), Spanish dagger, mesquite, coyotes, jack rabbits and chaparral birds can be thus classified. Of course there was the usual profusion of wild flowers, of all the hues that the rainbows use. But to an aspiring cowboy these were merely something to "cumbereth the earth," a source of embarrassment if not downright disgust. Consequently, only two of the species I came to identify, and identify with—the Indian pink and the buttercup—and these only for their utility. The middle pistil of the Indian pink, when plucked and sucked, gave off a delicious taste of honey. And the buttercup, just before it burst into bloom, gave off a soul-satisfying pop when dashed against someone else's forehead. (There was yet another useful flower identified, named, and classified, but due to the temper and the temperament of these times, its nickname, and use, cannot be revealed here.)

Flowers notwithstanding, it was God's country sure enough. Or at least a generous portion of it, most of which I could survey from our front gallery. Once I got big enough to climb the windmill I could see the rest of it, at the outer edge of which towered a giant Eclipse brand of windmill on top of King Mountain, fifteen miles to the southwest.

This portion of God's country sprawled across some thousand square miles of arid baldies and gentle swells, the northern half lapping over into the Great Staked Plains and the southern horizon rising into flat-topped mountains. With the exception of a few flocks of sheep under herd, Upton County was cow country. Those who ran both sheep and cattle had learned that in order to maintain one's dignity and self respect he must still run cattle. But to maintain himself with dignity—and maintain his cattle—he'd best run a flock or two of sheep.

During a land boom some years before, this sacred soil had felt the sting of nesters' plows, but these grangers soon starved out and drifted back down east, leaving the area one of the most thinly populated parts of the state. These departing squatters sold or leased their homesteads to ranchers who utilized the windmills and corrals but left the houses to wrack and ruin. These dilapidated shacks were to awake me to the horrible realization that God alone didn't ramrod this whole country. The devil also had a hand in it. This shattering bit of intelligence was passed down to me by my bigger brothers, Sog and Fush, while we were jostling along in the wagon on the road to JM headquarters. They let me in on a secret that was to haunt me for years to come.

"Paul, see that old nester shack yonder?" Fush asked.

"Yeah," I said, neither impressed or depressed.

"Well, it's hanted. Full of ghosts and boogers."

Profoundly moved, I looked over at my bigger brother for a word of denial, rebuttal, or refutation, preferably all three.

"Sure enough, Sog?"

"Sure enough!" he said, solemn as a sick owl. "Either that or rafters chuck full of crazy women!" (We always confused rafters and joists in those days.)

"Awwww. Bawwww. Boo hoo. Ahhhh."

"Now, dry up that bawlin', Paul," Sog said, glancing uneasily toward Papa up on the spring seat. "They won't bother you less'n you stir 'em up. Honest. Besides, they're just as a-skeered of you as you are of them?"

"How you know?"

"It's what the cowboys say."

That settled it. Settled it, that is, as regards the mutual horror established between myself and ghosts, haunts, and boogers. Cowboys knew it all. This I knew because Papa was one. And how I wish he could have overheard this dialog taking place in the back of the wagon. So he could have verified it just for the record. But I didn't dare relay this bit of intelligence to him—at least not in the presence of Sog and Fush.

"Why all crazy women up in them rafters, and no crazy men?"

"Men like it out here. And don't go crazy. Exceptin' sheepherders. Women don't, and they go loco from pure lonesome."

"Then, Sog, why don't crazy sheepherders take to the rafters?"

"They are afraid of women, crazy or not. Druther be took to jail. Besides, they don't like women nohow."

"Don't like women?" Fush put in. "Then they ain't as crazy as I thought."

"Ain't they no crazy men at all besides sheepherders?"

"No. Only a couple of really real wild ones. But you won't never ketch them in no rafters."

"Where do they stay at then?" I asked, alarmed again to the verge of bawling.

"Long ways from here," Sog assured me, glancing uneasily toward Papa. "One runs down in Tippitt's on the Pecos. The other'n —one with his throat cut from ear to ear and head hangin' back 'tween his shoulders—he runs west of here way over in the Y beef pasture."

"Sog," Fush put in, "you forgot about the JM ghost. The one that allus rides in on a white horse."

"We apt—apt to run across *him* on this trip?" I asked, my blood clabbering and my throat too constricted to bawl.

"Not 'less we stay till after dark," Sog reassured me—or thought he did. Ordinarily I would have pressed for details, but now I was too pressed for means by which to pry Papa loose from his augering the JM hands until dark, as was his custom.

CHAPTER III

Being the sixth child—"little for my age and dumb for my size," as Sog put it—I was a natural for the butt and brunt of Patterson horseplay. I bore and wore everything the older ones thrust upon me, from banter to britches and from derision to discarded drawers (which latter I could shed and shake off with ease). Would that I could have done as much for the constant badgering and baiting of the bigger ones. What with big brothers constantly and consistently springing at me from behind things, subjecting me to horror stories, ridiculing my speech and life styles, mine was an almost perpetual state of panic, insides constantly churned by turmoil, except for brief respites when Papa was home.

Even so, I loved and was proud of these Pattersons, all eight of them—nine including myself. Long before the advent of psychology per se I found them fascinating, if odd. First there was Papa, a medium-sized man of undeterminable age and somewhat of a stranger since he was away so much of the time hustling for our daily bread. Mostly, I remember his stern and steady blue eyes and the big bulging veins in his forearms which I mistook for muscles. In the house or out he wore a big white hat, uncreased, Indian style, not from eccentricity but to better shed water and to save wear and tear. Most of all I remember the big spurs that gave off sweet music when you twirled the rowels with a forefinger. These occasions were rare, however. Papa, not being one for show, only wore spurs, or boots, when the occasion demanded. How dull, drab, and dreary the habiliments of a freighter!

Yet, even in the drab unglamorous garb of a freighter, Papa was always welcome home for more reasons than one. Mainly because there was again law amongst the outlaws and consequently, for me, surcease from terror. Small wonder that I always cried inconsolably when he left, knowing that this sorrow would soon be replaced by horror—a horror hatched up in the fertile minds of Sog and Fush.

Then there was Mama to whom my every wish was an executed order. And whither Mama went, there went I, scarcely allowing her the privacy of the privy. To me Mama was the epitome of brilliance, beauty, and good grooming. But in time I was to discover that this was only partially the case. Brilliant, yes, and beautiful, but well-groomed only when Aunt Embelle Pollard came down and fixed her up. (But, doggone it, Aunt Embelle had no business fixing us kids up too!)

Then came Ralph, the first born, a dim and distant figure who was more like an uncle, since he lived with Grandad and Grandma Pollard up north somewhere. Next was Blanche who was more like a mother since she shouldered most of the household responsibilities. She was the first to really impress me, and it was her extreme bravery rather than the invaluable services she rendered. In addition to rescuing me from drowning in the tank, she had only recently walked the wagon tongue, calmly retrieved the dragging lines, and circled a runaway team by Papa, so he could pull them to a stop. It was like Fush said: "Blanche, she can ride a horse a-runnin'. Or maybe even a-pitchin'. And her only a girl to boot."

Sog (John around company), in spite of his proneness to panic-strike me, was my favorite of the bunch. When the notion struck him he could tell stories as funny as he could tell them scary. And already he was showing signs of making a cowboy—the only calling on God's green earth worthy of considering at all.

Madge was next, but like Ralph, seemed a distant relative. She too had been adopted by the Pollards. I did have a dim recollection of her being pretty, which made her seem even more so when I learned she was my sister.

Fush, a year and a half my senior, was best known to me, what with acting alternately as my adviser, chastiser, mentor, tormenter, and, finally, protector when the need arose. At times I felt that he defended me against strange, mean kids only because he regarded me as his exclusive pick-on property. Fush was of a temper (and temperament) the boogerman himself could not have disturbed, or perturbed. That is unless the old bad man himself had threatened to do me bodily harm. As aforesaid, bodily harm was Fush's exclusive right. But mostly, especially with Sog gone, life with Fush could be exciting, to say the least. And, unfortunately, it could also be downright dangerous.

Only Papa (with his spurs on) projected a more exciting image than Fush and him barefooted, stick-straight, and just as skinny. He had a pick-handle build, head and all (Ralph's description). From this pick-handle head sprang a wild growth of straw-straight, straw-colored hair. And before he took the top half of one of Blanche's lisle stockings and trained this mop to "pompadour" it bristled like a mad mus' hog's. And underneath those bristles bristled limitless ideas on how to court death without actually consummating the vows of matrimony, that is, how to look the Angel of Death square in the eye and make Him avert his face.

Gwen, the last one, was still a babe in arms, too young to have developed individuality, I figured. Even so, she was bright and walking upright, with a mouth full of teeth and clever sayings at an age when I was still all gums and thumbs and traveling on all fours. On top of that she was usurping attention and services which, I felt, were wholly and solely mine.

Gwen (or Nig or Pots) was to hold a unique and solitary place amongst all Pattersons in that she was the only one to acquire two nicknames. Nig was the name that stuck with all except Papa and

Mama. Mama held doggedly to Gwendolyn whereas Papa always referred to this last child as Pots. Not that the three-letter nickname was meant as a disparagement to another race—at least not in our household, as none of us ever heard either parent speak disparagingly of any race, creed, or color. In fact, I was five years old before I ever beheld a black man. This was Prince Albert, ex-cowboy of considerable renown and currently wagon cook for the 7H, who held the admiration and respect of all colors and creeds.

However, in deference to a supersensitive society I shall scrupulously shun this nonobscene, nonprofane three-letter word that is nowadays so offensive. What's more I shall likewise shun those obscene, profane four-letter words that, ironically, are no longer offensive to today's supersensitive society. So, hereafter I shall refer to our little sister as Gwen, not even hazarding the word Pots for fear it might now be numbered among the offensives.

Not to be overlooked was old Philip, our dog, who was a Patterson through and through—optimistic, generous, gullible among city dogs and ever rearing to head for the horizon and the hills beyond. Old Philip was an average-sized black and white canine of questionable, if varied, ancestry. Dog of pedigree, dog of low degree, dog of no degree, who knows? But from somewhere old Philip had inherited qualities to be prized in both man and beast: indomitable courage, with scrapping skill to match, loyalty, honesty, integrity, and perseverance in the face of great adversity. He favored neither the Pattersons nor the Pollards, but for sheer strength of character he was more like Fush (except he was much kinder to me). In fact he and Fush were inseparable companions except on cold nights when Fush had to come inside. Here there had to be a parting because of Papa's peculiar idea about bringing up boys and dogs.

CHAPTER IV

The call to general quarters aboard a battleship in hostile waters, or the cry of "fire" in a crowded theater couldn't have triggered more action or engendered greater pandemonium than Papa's bolt-out-of-the-blue announcement: "Get a move on, wife, you kids, we're a drivin' into Upland."

The male element scattered like a covey of quail, diving under beds for hats, bolting to the windmill for lost shoes, scrambling under the house for misplaced stockings, squeezing behind the bureau for shirts.

The female element, with everything in place, merely had to move to the bureau mirror and start primping. Even so, the male element was loaded on and goading the distaff side to "hurry up, for gosh sakes!" Upland, where we had blown our last seventy-five cents for a grubstake, more than compensated for nester shack rafters full of crazy women and a pasture full of wild men, plus a couple of hants thrown in. No traveler from Marco Polo on down could have looked forward with greater anticipation than we did toward this trip to Upland.

We had been there once before, but that didn't count. We were flat broke, it was drizzling rain, and Papa had made us stay in the wagon. What's more, the wagon sheet, though flimsy, wouldn't allow for taking in the sights. On top of that I was still within that period of life when the earth was without form and void.

So, ever since our arrival some five months ago, that stately green cupola of the courthouse two miles to our west continued to beckon like the siren's call. So much so that it had become to us what, I imagine, that Pagoda was to Kipling's Tommy "On the Road to Mandalay." Now, if we weren't dreaming, it was about to yield up its mysteries—outside mysteries, at least. We doubted that Papa would let us prowl around inside.

The buggy, which came with the Taylor place, was no more than a snug two-passenger, but would very well serve for a seven-seater in this case—that is if three crouched down on the floor board and two stood in back. So, with Papa and Mama on the seat, Blanche and Sog standing in the back, and Fush, Gwen, and me sardined down in front, our chins wedged over the dashboard we headed for the thrill of our lives. Not a very favorable position for us dashboarders, what with faces constantly switched by horse tails and our keen noses, and fine sensibilities, subject to whatever embarrassing urge the horses might be struck with. Not a position conducive to harmony. Even so, Fush and I made the entire trip without so much as exchanging a single blow or yanking a single hank of hair. Too great an event to risk missing.

Across the years it has been my good fortune to savor the sights, sounds, and smells of this world's major cities, both foreign and domestic. All "vanity and vexation of spirit" compared to that first over-the-horse-rump view of Upland, Texas (population fifty-odd, counting the cow ponies and one lone hound-dog) shimmering in the golden sunshine. The chimes of London's Big Ben, the deep-voiced bonging of the ten-foot bronze Mori of the torre dell' Orlogio on St. Mark's Square in Venice, the tolling of temple bells the length and breadth of Spain and Old Mexico—all "as sounding brass and tinkling cymbals" compared to the ring and sing of cowboy spurs in Upland that day. Ditto for the rest of the world's sights and smells.

Enclosed by a red wooden fence towered the great two-story stone courthouse with its high, green dome, a flat-topped rock jail, a tall red windmill flanked by two red cypresswood tanks on towers. Inside the fence all around marched neatly-rowed, stately mulberry trees in full leaf. (Doggone it. No mulberries yet, even if Papa, apt as not, wouldn't let us fly into them.)

Outside the red fence lay a long red water trough for the buggy and saddle stock. This fence was likewise equipped with stiles at strategic spots and with hitch racks at which were hitched the two broncs and a whole row of seasoned, settled cow ponies. Which meant, of course, *cowboys in town*. Also, farther down the fence another bunch of saddled ponies, standing hipshot, their reins on the ground. Which meant more cowboys in town. And anchored to mesquites here and there stood three or four wall-eyed buggy teams. Like Granddad Pollard peeking over his specs they peered around the bridle blinds, seeking the faintest excuse to strew buggy accessories across the rolling plains.

Skirting the courthouse square on four sides was a handful of wooden buildings, but no garage or filling station, what with horse-power still chiefly in the horse. The machine age was beginning to make its encroachments, however, for there were a couple of horse-less carriages in the vicinity—John Garner's Cole 8 and old Dutch Henry's E. M. F. But in deference to the fractious ponies (and their more fractious owners, perhaps) these fearsome vehicles were hitched too far away for us to tell anything about. And Papa wasn't one to let his kids prowl around other people's property.

"Papa, where you reckon all them cowboys are at"? This would be Fush, of course.

"Over in the Mercantile, I expect."

"Then let's hurry and get over there."

"Hold your horses. That's right where we're a-headin'."

Fush couldn't keep his eye off our destination but, enthralled as I was with cowboys, I couldn't help but take in the other sights en route. I perceived that three hundred yards from the courthouse square in any direction the city limits quit off and cow country set in, that is, except for a white building on the slope of a hill some three quarters of a mile to the southwest.

"That's the schoolhouse," Blanche put in, "where me and Sog hope to be from now on."

"Where you get that there me-and-Sog stuff? I aim to get on 'study' with the JM's, come summer."

"Hold your horses, Soggum. You ain't that big yet," this from Papa.

Diagonally across from the courthouse loomed John R. Johnston's General Mercantile to which we were headed (and far too slow, I figured). Once there we glommed the place, pounced in upon it just as soon as Papa and our floor-board cramped legs would permit.

There they were. All of them. The cowboys (all of whom we'd missed on our trip to the JM's) lounging against the counter, sitting cross-legged upon it, some eating canned peaches with their pocket knives, some rolling Bull Durham cigarettes and one or two testing John R's quirts, bridle reins, and girts.

Via the grapevine, or by some mysterious affinity with his kind, Fush already knew them. Not on speaking terms yet, as were Papa and Sog, but one by one he whispered their names: "The great big one there with the boot hat, that's Charley Lyons. He's bound to be the one on the roan bronc. That one yonder, the one with the brass-studded cuffs on, the bronc belt and the bandanner, he's Lewis Phillips. He looks wild enough to be the one on that other bronc, but he ain't. This 'n over here is Joe Lane, he's apt to be forkin' the other bronc. Him or that 'un, Guy McLaughlin. The one just finishin' his peach juice is J. C. Jackson, the other big one is Bill Atkins. And that one talkin' to Papa is Lee Reynolds. And if you ain't heard tell of Lee Reynolds you've got no business here —or anywheres else."

Who was this Lee Reynolds that Fush put above Charley Lyons? Anybody saltier than the man forking that wall-eyed roan must be somebody come, sure enough. I moved over to see. Lee was a blocky little cowboy with a reddish-gray mustache and steady, deep-blue eyes. He was wearing a neat black Stetson uncreased like Papa's, a neat blue vest, California pants, shop-made boots and medium-sized, silver-mounted spurs, but no leggin's like the other cowboys. Not overdressed like Lewis Phillips, yet not slouchy like the stranger Fush couldn't place. Not much to look at compared to Charley Lyons. So what was the magnetism? Lee Reynolds was somebody to listen to, then, judging from the crowd gravitating around him and Papa.

"Well, Lee, how's it goin' "? Papa asked. (Bound for Papa. He too was great for conversation. People gravitated around him too. But whereas Lee was probably the finest talker in the country, Papa was given up to be the finest listener.)

"Things're shapin' up, Pat," Lee was saying, "things keep runnin' this-a-way one day I'll be a rich man—a million days a million dollars!"

By this time the cowboys had finished their peaches and their purchases and were jingling out, Fush at their heels, faunching to see them mount up and ride off. This was my intention also, but suddenly I caught myself standing spellbound by my surroundings, their smells first, then their sights—the exotic aroma of cheese, bacon, new saddle leather, pickles, crackers, lightbread, calico, neat's-foot oil, coal oil, bananas. Undoubtedly the supply base for the world. With my own eyes I was seeing John R. rummage around behind piles of saddle blankets, horseshoe kegs, sacked potatoes, and fish out every need—and want—of mankind.

Completely oblivious to the mill and melee about me I stood transfixed at the shelved canned goods with their brilliant labels of red, red tomatoes, golden peaches, purple plums, and so on. But from the six-bits-worth-of-staples episode, I realized, with sinking heart, that such delicacies were as unobtainable as the moon—except on credit, which mode of operation was completely foreign to Papa's life style. Canned goods were the "fancies" mentioned on

John R's General Mercantile sign. Poor people like the Patterson's were strictly limited to staples, such as, sowbelly and molasses, for which latter we sought status by labeling them "double-breasted ham" and "syrup."

Depressed by the brutal realities, I switched back into my old familiar fantasies—the cowboys, how they acted, dressed, and so on. Strangely, I hadn't noticed it before, but suddenly I recalled that practically all of them—Lee Reynolds and Charley Lyons especially—had Bull Durham tobacco tags dangling from their vest or breast pockets. Just then, by some odd coincidence, my eye fell on a castaway Bull Durham sack, its beautiful round tag intact. The badge of a cowboy. Lord only knows when I would own some boots (or even shoes) or spurs or leggin's, or even a vest. But as of right now I could own me a Bull Durham sack, tag and all! Oh, I knew I'd been taught not to pick up stuff, regardless of its worth, or its worthlessness. But this one had been cast away. Nobody on God's green earth would want it or would have any earthly use for it. Except me. I felt guilty enough to catch everybody looking off, but without the teeniest twinge of conscience I nipped up the sack and, casually, as I figured Charley Lyons would do it, made as if to put it in my breast pocket. Doggone it, I wished now that I had worn the despised little sailor blouse with the girl-like collar behind. But it did have a breast pocket. How could a man ever commence to look like a cowboy without a breast pocket. The best I could do was stuff the thing down my shirt front with the tag hanging out. On second thought, I'd best leave the whole thing inside till I got to the privacy of behind the barn. And maybe there'd be enough tobacco left for me to roll me one. What a cowboy picture I would present to Fush. Not only with a Bull Durham tag hanging out but a cigarette dangling from my lips to boot!

But back in the buggy the behind-the-barn scene seemed too remote and far away. Fush must get his impression now. So, I snuck out the tag and let it dangle, Charley-Lyons-like, down the front of my shirt. Fush was immediately, and duly, impressed, amazed. But so was Papa with his X-ray eyes!

"Young man, where'd you get that sack?"

"Back yonder," I said in a voice barely audible from a *being* barely visible, such was my shrinkage into the floor board.

"Back where yonder?"

"In the mercantile store," I murmured weakly, "on the floor, back behind the pertaters."

Papa had already turned the buggy around and was high-tailing it back to Upland.

"Young man," I could feel Papa's auger eyes boring clean through the back of my head, "you take that sack back and lay it down exactly—I mean exactly—where you got it. Savvy"?

"Yes—yes, sir."

"And you tell Mr. Johnston you got it and you want to put it back. Savvy"?

"Ye—yes, sir."

That trip to the back of the Mercantile was the longest walk of my life, but not nearly as long as the speech I had to make to John R, even if I did manage to take some of the sting out of it.

"Mr. Johnston, I found this tobacker sack in the back of the store—it was plumb slap dab empty but Papa said back there was where it belongs." I was too long gone to get John R's reply. However, the trip out, though at full speed, turned out still longer when I began to ponder what Papa might do next. But for a change and for a wonder he never brought up the subject again. (Neither did I.) A memorable comeuppance, but not enough to dim the luster of that trip to Upland.

CHAPTER V

It was here at the Taylor place that little personalities began to blossom, to crystalize. As was predictable, Fush was blossoming into an adventurer with some characteristics of the realist and the practical man. On the other hand, I was drifting farther into daydreamland. Already I was an unabashed passivist, not to say pacifist. While Fush was out riding the milk stock, hanging by his toes from the windmill tower, trying to grab onto the tails of wild range cattle as they came in to water, and seeking other means whereby he could defy death, I was content to lie in the shade of the wild china and relive, via flashback, my close brushes with danger. Even before the age of accountability, I could recall vividly the close calls of my past. While Fush was ever probing the present for perils, I was content to derive my thrills from those episodes of the past. Examples:

The time over at the K. C. M. & O. section house when I lay on the track, ear glued to the rail, completely mesmerized by the clackety-clack of an oncoming train. In the nick of time Papa had snatched me from the iron jaws (or wheels) of death. The mangling I received at Papa's hands was only slightly less than what a fast freight could have ministered. Fine way for a father to demonstrate love! This experience sent Papa in search of move number fifteen and another job. "Strictly," Sog said, "to keep me from getting my fool head squashed off one of these days."

And down at Salt Well that time when a wild bull jumped the dipping vat and took after me, huffing and snuffing at the nakedness under my shirt tail for what seemed like a couple of eternities, but was actually only a couple of jumps. Just long enough, Sog says, for the old bull to realize he was completely outclassed as a racer. And the time Blanche fished me out of the bottom of the Kircheville tank after I had tried to walk on water. This attempt to emulate our Lord came about after I had tried to rescue my stick horse that Fush had thrown in. This was by no means an act of faith or of valor on my part but an act of stupidity. The moss-covered surface appeared to me like solid ground.

This thirst for thrills satisfied, this yen for danger thus appeased, I would turn to dreams best suited to my make-up—picturing in my mind's eye the Pattersons heading Uplandwards on brand new bicycles, all strung out in a line, headlights cutting golden swaths through the darkness just as pictured in Sears & Roebuck. Papa in the lead, then Mama and so on down to little Gwen. Well, maybe she ought to be on a tricycle, which would certainly be more in our price range at $1.25. And come to think of it, Papa and Mama ought to be in a new buggy, $25.95 (topless) which would beat that $13.60 for bicycles. Better still, I would have everyone on horseback, but even my resilient imagination couldn't stretch that far. Seven head of horses was more than three times the size our horse herd ever *was, is* or, quite likely, ever *shall be.*

The Sears catalog, doubtless, was partially responsible for my imagination developing out of proportion to the rest of me. How full it was of saddles, bicycles, cowboy suits, three-bladed knives, six-shooters, and rifles—things that could be possessed with the mind's eye! Why wear one's self out playing with rag baseballs and wagon-spoke bats, as Fush did, when a veritable sesame existed closer than hands and feet? All one had to do was open the "look book" and there it was.

What's more this agile imagination had a way of converting nights into nightmares. In cahoots with Sog and Fush, it transformed a common fence post into the Tippitt wild man; converted a Spanish dagger into somebody right out of a nester's rafters. Under its influence every greasewood bush became a skulking human form. It produced a night wind that chilled the very blood with its ghostlike wails and caused owls to screech like crazy women.

Result: an almost perpetual state of inner pandemonium, except when Papa was around. Papa was insurance against anything, anytime, anywhere, including the wiles of the devil, not to mention those of Sog and Fush. Papa was insurance against a rooster crowing at night and a hen crowing by day or night. To me these were the most terrible of omens, a sure and certain sign of a death in the family. Grandma Patterson would immediately take a night-crowing rooster and a day-crowing hen and wring their necks. Yes, Papa most assuredly was insurance against all evil, most especially against the wiles of the devil. As a consequence, the devil never dared lay a hand on me, though he tempted, prompted, and instigated Fush into so doing at every opportunity.

I, the idealist, and Fush, the realist, were developing ambitions in common, however. We aspired to become cowboys. Consequently we were developing similar tastes in clothes. Our sartorial preferences ran along the line of high, wide, and handsome Stetsons, leather cuffs, spotted sleeve holders and big, loud-voiced spurs. And, of course, vests or shirts with Bull Durham pockets against that far and distant day when we might be allowed to utilize the stuff.

Papa, however, continued to dictate the fashion—or lack of it. We were restricted—under extreme duress—to unshirtlike blouses, rag hats, snap-brim straws (which we called turtle-tops), buster brown shoes in season (which was seldom), and bloomer britches with elastic waistband instead of belt and a flap instead of a buttoned fly. Needless to say this get up got us down and caused us no end of anguish and embarrassment. Our chief source of humilia-tion should have been but, oddly enough, wasn't, the inevitably faulty flap that had a habit of betraying one's nakedness on the most inopportune of occasions.

So abhorrent were these monstrosities that one day I swore to forego the Sears section on saddles and turned to page 1090 to "OUR GREAT ASSORTMENT OF LITTLE FELLOWS' WASHABLE SUITS" and got Blanche to read me what Sears had to say about them. Surely they couldn't have anything compli-mentary about such a get up. What Blanche read me most nigh shattered my faith in Papa and Mama's sanity—if not in their sanity, at least in their judgment. They had been buying us $1.00 sailor suits (with flaps) when they could have been buying us well made little garments *which button with a fly*, for thirty-eight cents! What is more they could have bought us a blue and white cham-bray suit (with fall-out proof fly) sporting outside breast pocket *and cord and whistle* for forty-five cents.

"Fush, why you reckon they don't furnish a cord and whistle with that dollar suit?" I asked, disconsolate.

"Lordy, I'm glad they don't."

"Lordy, why?" I asked, now questioning Fush's judgment, if not his sanity.

"Whistle, and call attention to one's self in a get up like that? Not on your life. 'Specially as tricky as them D——g flaps are."

"I see," I said, abhorring myself and repenting in dust and ashes.

Although our cross was rugged and our yoke continued heavy we managed to bear them, that is until a little kid out of a place called Midland dropped by dressed in a full-grown cowboy out-fit—from Stetson hat to long britches clean on down to spurs and shop-made boots! We still had to bear the yoke but it was seven times seventy more galling.

More despicable even than the faulty-flap bloomers were those turtle-top straws—and far more likely to attract unfavorable atten-tion than anything that could happen to us below the belt, or rather the elastic waistband. What rejoicing, what unconfined joy, when these straws were eaten by a cow or spirited away (with our subtle assistance) by a passing whirlwind. Papa soon put a quietus on this racket, however. He commenced buying us straws rendered inedible by a vile-smelling varnish of some sort, and he equipped them with twine string throat latches.

CHAPTER VI

Here at the Taylor place the West unfolded in one complete, panoramic picture and not just shreds and patches such as the bull jumping over the dipping vat down at Salt Well, or the four shadowy horsemen driving a phantom herd over in Reagan County. The Taylor place was equipped with horse-breaking corrals (complete with snubbing post), and right now one of the Midland Taylors and another cowboy were fixing to snap out a couple of wild ones.

"Can me and Paul stay and watch?" Fush asked.

"Why, shore," said Taylor, "stick around till the show's over."

"Will it ever start?" Fush whispered, impatient at the endless "sacking," bucking out with the saddle, and the jerking and chousing at the end of a hackamore rope. The action-prone Fush was an advocate of Uncle Fisher Pollard's method of bronc skinning. His system was simple—tie up a hind foot, buckle on the old kack, let the foot down, have a couple of stout hands ear the critter and step upstairs. While the poor old bronc still had some "show" in him.

"Shucks, Paul, I'm goin' in the house and look at Indians and cowboys on the stereoscope, where the action's at."

Fush was just fixing to fit his action to the word when the other cowboy spoke up. Not what the cowboy said, but how he said it was what brought us both up short.

"Taylor, whyn't ye get ye a ne—ne—new saiddleeeeeeeeeee?" The way he half-howled, half-growled it, we didn't know whether to snicker or run; but since the cowboy had already turned back to the "sacking" of his bronc, we settled on the former.

"I never heard anything like it in my whole life," I said in an aside to Fush, "not even in Uncle Josh's *Laughing Stories* we heard on Aunt Zo's graphophone!"

It was a case where words spoke louder than action, but after that one utterance the show was done over in both word and deed. Not another word out of the strange cowboy and not a jump from the broncs. Even so, it turned out a most memorable day. So much so that "Taylor whyn't ye ge—g—get ye a ne—ne—new saiddleeeeeeeee?" became a byword that can be heard amongst us to this day.

Words-speaking-louder-than-action notwithstanding, our first cowboys at work lessened our resolve to become cowboys not one jot nor tittle. Besides, here at the Taylor place range cattle would water in bunches, bulls would fight, and eventually they gathered a herd and held it right out in front of our house—stood guard one night, just like Papa used to do, working for old Col. C. C. Slaughter up on the plains.

In charge of this herd was Mr. Schnaubert, Upland's first sheriff. Fush and I were a little disappointed to learn that Mr. Schnaubert hadn't taken this herd away from rustlers, like they did in that magic lantern show Sog was telling us about. Even so, there was plenty of thrill left. And what a comfort it was at bedtime—for a change—to know that not three hundred yards away a herd was bedded down, with cowboys circling same as on the long trail drives we'd heard Granddad Pollard tell about. This smell and bawl of cattle was perfume to our nostrils and music to our ears. For sure, cowboying would be our calling, our career, our life's work, that is if Papa would ever buy us the proper style hats. A man could never cowboy in a turtle-topped straw—couldn't look a cow in the eye, much less a cowboy.

How faithful to duty, how loyal all cowboys were, duty in spite of danger, h——l or high water. Rub tobacco juice in their eyes to stay awake. Ever trustworthy, ever alert, never known to falter or fail. Oh, how bitterly disappointed I was to be. And how soon! Next morning they told us that John Miller had gone to sleep on guard and fallen off his horse. Everybody laughed except me—and Mr. Schnaubert. Well, at least two cowboys in the crowd, I thought to myself sadly. Nevertheless, this shameful spectacle of John Miller falling asleep and, subsequently, off his horse, though disillusioning, would not deter us from joining that fraternity at the earliest possible date.

Shortly, our burning zeal to cowboy took on added spark when Papa showed up one day with the report that he had got on with a trail herd bound for an outfit to the tip top of the Texas Panhandle. However, the edge was dulled considerably when we learned that Papa had signed on as cook! If the dose was bitter for me it was doubly so for Fush. To me, the dreamer, it meant only that Papa would miss out on the wild night stampedes with ball lightning playing between a thousand sets of horns, the topping off of mean horses, perhaps. And on night guards where he'd have to use his Tinsley seepings for something besides antidotes for our ant and wasp stings. To Fush, the man of action, the realist, the practical one, it meant not only missing out on all these thrills, but it caused him no little concern over whether Papa could hold down his job. Cooking? Trail outfits, he'd heard, fed good—stashed in all sorts of "staples" plus plenty of "fancies" to prepare. And Papa was experienced only in the preparation of sowbelly, baking powder biscuits, flour gravy, and sugar molasses!

CHAPTER VII

Papa so long gone and so far away brought out a new side to Mama. Well, not necessarily a new side, just the old side more pronounced—scarier than ever, especially at night. She not only saw the things I saw in my wildest imaginings but she began to hear voices, which development didn't seem to faze Fush but forced me to share my anxiety over Papa's well-being with being scared with, and about, Mama. But, surprisingly, Mama turned out more resourceful than Fush and myself combined. One morning she announced, right out of a clear sky, "Chil'ern, we're going to your Grandma Pollard's," which chopped off Fush's brooding over Papa and my brooding-worrying at one fell swoop.

"When, Mama?" Fush's and my shrill, thrilled voices, practically in unison.

"In the morning."

"Where's Grandma at, Mama?"

"Other side of Andrews."

"Where's Andrews at?"

"Other side of Midland!"

"Where's Midland at?"

"Pose your questions correctly, chil'ern, and I'll commence answering them," Mama snapped, in a rare show of temper. "What I mean is, leave off that *at*." Indifferent in her dress, perhaps, slipshod in her cooking, and careless in her housework—and at times her pronunciation of the word "children"—Mama was ever a stickler for correct grammar in those days, a throwback to her "elecution" tutoring days back in Buffalo Gap.

"Okay, so where's Midland a——?"

"About fifty miles north."

"Where's north?"

"I get my directions confused. Let Blanche and John tell you when they get home from school."

"Fifty miles. Golleeeeeeee bum!" Fush said.

I had not the slightest conception of how far fifty miles was but judging from Fush's expletive—the very strongest he was permitted to use—it must be plumb to another world.

"Then how far on to Andrews?"

"Another forty, I expect. And your Grandma Pollard's is still another fifteen miles beyond that."

This last bit of information from Mama was met with complete, absolute silence. There was just no expletive to cover the magnitude of such an undertaking, to cope with such a scope of distance. For a clear picture we would have to wait until Blanche and Sog got home. The former, a specialist in geography, and the latter, a mathematician of sorts, could pinpoint our destination and compute the miles.

"Fifty, sixty miles. Then forty, then fifteen more! Fush, that can't be got to from here, can it?" I asked, a brand new brooding, now full blown, replacing both the old brooding over Papa and the old fear with Mama.

"If it's there, old Bullet and Humpy can get us to it," he assured me.

"Yes, but what if old Humpy gives us the slip? He's pure de *mus*tang, you remember," I went on, surging tide of enthusiasm suddenly overrun by a passel of new fears and phobias, which I concealed from Fush. Or thought I did.

"I know what you're thinkin'. Old Humpy he can hide in a

clump of brush no bigger than he is and can sneak along without jingling the bell around his neck—not one teeny tinkle. But Sog will stake him and hobble him to boot," Fush said, strangely charitable toward the fears and phobias that were reasserting themselves in me.

"But what if they run away with the wagon like they did that time down at the Johnston place?"

"Blanche'll circle 'm down. Just like last time."

"But what if the wagon tires roll off?"

"They won't. Sog'll pull into a water hole and soak 'em first."

"But ain't we too little to go that far without Papa?"

"Blanche is not. Nor Sog. Me neither—nor you, even. Little Gwen, maybe, but Blanche and Mama'll keep care of her."

"And me too," I would have added, but for fear of being shamed as "itty bitty titty baby," which was Fush's favorite silencer.

CHAPTER VIII

Once the old narrow-tired Rock Island began to roll it not only proved a balm to my wanderlust but an antidote to my broodings and fears. Now all that remained was a faint, unnamed anxiety against the awesome stretch ahead—the sort of anxiety that must have assailed Columbus, say, or Marco Polo. (But then neither was working the likes of old Humpy.) And, by the time we had pulled through Upland, the last faint trace of apprehension had been dispelled. Although Papa had seen to it that we were left with plenty of "staples," we had prevailed upon Blanche, our purchasing agent, to pull in at General Mercantile and stock up on "fancies." "What will Papa say?" had been her argument, but her defense was hopeless, helpless against what we were saying *now*.

"All right, then, Sog and me'll go get them," Blanche had said. They had quit the wagon simultaneously, in too big a rush almost to wrap the lines around a wheel hub.

"Me and Paul too," Fush had said, the both of us poised to jump.

"No, you don't." The command could well have been Papa's, stern and no-foolishness-like as it was. But it had come from Mama. The double shock of it immobilized us, froze us in our tracks.

That great supply of fancies Blanche was supposed to stow in turned out to be a loaf of lightbread, two cans of pork and beans, and a can of peaches. Fush and I, not realizing that our stomachs could be so much bigger than our eyes, were elated to the extreme. Thus plenteously provisioned, who cared if old Humpy did slip his hobbles? Or a tire rolled off? Or we got lost? But in the face of six ravenous, "fancy"-starved appetites the lightbread, the peaches and most of the pork and beans disappeared that first night in camp.

"Mama, where's the pork at?" Fush, of course.

"It had done disappeared to start with," Sog put in, even before Mama had time to take off his *at*.

No sooner had the lightbread, peaches, the pork and practically all the beans disappeared until old Humpy went and did likewise, taking old Bullet with him. Rushing into the void they had created were all the old frights, fears, and alarms that my flesh was ever heir to. Here I was, left to starve on the plains or to be set upon by Brahma bulls or lobo wolves or carried off by crazy women or wild men.

"Doggone old Humpy. I could cut his throat with a widder woman's pocket knife," as Papa would have put it. And doggone Papa. He might not have furnished us lightbread and other goodies, but he could have come along and furnished us protection on this trip. Sog, however, furnished a fair-to-middlin' substitute for Papa even if the kid was but eleven years old. He trailed the sneakaways, brought them back, and had the old Rock Island rolling again by ten o'clock.

What with wheels chuckling under me again and trace chains ringing out their siren song, all was forgiven, forgotten. There was something solid, substantial, reassuring about rolling wheels, something that put God back in his Heaven and all right with the world. This era of good feeling continued all through that day and on up into the night, pitch darkness notwithstanding. I lay, round-eyed, under the tarp, lulled by the friendly night sounds and smells, certain sure that God up there on his star-spangled throne was looking down, and our prospects were looking up.

From up there He was just fixing to direct His prairie orchestra which was now tuning up for the night. Put me in mind of fiddlers tuning up for an all-night dance—only much prettier than dance fiddling. Out yonder a couple of old coyotes (or a dozen—it was hard to tell) were running through their *do re mi's.* And back here a night bird of some sort was blowing himself a few notes—not a kildee, thank goodness. The call of a kildee was most nigh as spooky as a rooster crowing after sundown. From some direction, or all directions, came the steady drone of crickets, their song punctuated occasionally by the snapping and crackling of a dead mesquite stump on the fire. Blanche had buried a molasses bucket with perforated top, and when the stump was reduced to coals she was going to shovel them over the top so tomorrow we could have beans, frijole beans, not as fancy as the long-gone pork and beans, but more stable.

Not a sour note in God's prairie orchestra, not even the mournful sighing of the wind through the draw ropes of the wagon sheet, nor the flapping of Blanche's cup towel fastened to a sideboard. Not even Sog tumbling and mumbling in his sleep. But what if amongst the strains of this sweet music there should bust out the hoarse and hungry cry of a lobo wolf? All the old fears and horrors were about to stampede through me when I caught the *ruck, ruck, ruck* of old Philip scratching fleas and I was off into the land of dreams.

CHAPTER IX

"Let's swing by your Aunt Hallie's and Uncle Will's out from Garden City a ways," Mama announced right out of a clear spring sky. It was news that set well with my breakfast—flapjacks, double-breasted ham and sugar molasses. (To make the meal complete I utilized my well-developed powers of imagination to conjure up a plate of pork and beans for dessert.) I was especially elated at Mama's announcement, not to say greatly relieved. The Midland road was edged occasionally with thick mesquite mottes and flanked with that natural habitat for hants and boogers—abandoned nesters' shacks. The Garden City direction, on the other hand, was mile upon mile of open baldies—visibility unlimited and thus insurance against old Humpy sneaking off from us or anything sneaking up.

This change of itinerary likewise was met with approval by all except Sog. He voiced no reason for his reluctance but he didn't have to. In taking roundance upon mesquite mottes and nesters' shacks he would be handicapped somewhat in finding something with which to petrify the pants off of me. You could almost hear the schemes, plots, and subterfuges roiling and boiling inside his head.

"Paul, want to jump out and help Fush and old Philip chouse prairie dogs and chunk cow chips at screech owls?"

"Unh unh."

"You're afraid of prairie dogs and screech owls."

"UNH UNH."

"Then why ain't you out and after 'em?"

I refused to answer that one. Not only on the grounds that it might tend to intimidate me, but simply because we both knew what he had in mind—whip up the team and leave me like the poor cowboy in the song, to die on the lone prairie. This challenge met and conquered, the sing of trace chains and the chuckle of wheels soon lulled me into a sense of serenity, a state of security. But could it last with somebody like Sog in the driver's seat? As if in answer to my unvoiced question, the flat plain was beginning to give way to gentle swells, which cut visibility to only a mile or so. It was as if the very earth itself was conspiring with that villain in the driver's seat. Even then my sense of serenity wouldn't have suffered a setback but for a big wooden gate that suddenly loomed across the road ruts. The gate itself wasn't scary and couldn't have concealed a booger behind its wide-spaced planks. But thereon was scrawled a message—a message Sog solemnly read aloud as he handed Blanche the lines and got out to open up.

"The Road to Hell!"

"Sure enough, is that what it says, Blanche?"

Blanche, stricken by my stricken countenance, obviously tried to cover up, tried to scan the message silently. But she was a lip reader, which tended to confirm the terrifying news. Except for this, I might have dismissed it as another one of Sog's pranks.

"H—how far, you reckon, Blanche?"

Preoccupied with driving through the gate, plus the fact that my voice was reduced by terror to a strangled whisper, Blanche missed the question. But it was picked up by the keen-eared Sog as we went by.

"How far to hell? I'd say, like old Wash Forbes does that 'Hell ain't a halfa mile from here.'"

"John, you shouldn't devil the child." Mama's rebuke, meant to still my fears, only added brimstone to the fire. What with my present state the devil fitted right in.

"Ai—isn't they no way around it? No other road?"

"You don't see none, do you?" Sog asked, the 360-degree sweep of his arm taking in nothing but two endless ruts.

But for the fact that my constitution—the psyche, they call it now—had become almost inured to pandemonium and was forever getting the call to general quarters, I would have expired on the spot, to fill an early grave on the lone prairie. Which, on second thought, would have been preferable to rolling on a few hundred yards further and dropping into hell.

"Where, wh—what'll happen next?"

"Why, right over that next little rise, the wagon'll jist fall right in, I expect," Sog said, pointing ahead with the butt end of the whip handle.

Suddenly I found that some of the panic had left me—shoved aside by a strange resentment. There we were on the road to hell, and Fush and old Philip out running their fool heads off after prairie dogs. Now the strange resentment was being contested by a streak of decency, of loyalty to both Fush and old Philip. Ought I to call out and warn them away or just call them in and let them go to hell with the rest of us?

Thus caught between the horns of such a dilemma I had nothing left to do but resort to the usual. Which I did, and in that bleating, grating key that always got results. Blanche, moved either by genuine sympathy or quicked to the quick in a sympathetic nerve, interceded in my behalf. She finally, and mostly, convinced me that Sog was only fooling, and the gate was only fooling too. Even so, I didn't let all my weight down until we had passed through another gate which she assured me was the one leading out the other side.

"How do you know?" I asked, still skeptical.

"Well," Sog put in, "don't you figure you jist been through hell?"

I readily admitted that I had.

38

CHAPTER X

The visit at Uncle Will's and Aunt Hallie's was an experience so real that it now seemed beyond the realm of reality—something more like one of my daydreams. Real ranch, real horses, real cattle, and real grub—staple and fancy. And they were the real owners, not just living on it like we were on the Taylor place. All this plus a real automobile which was, sad to say, broke down at the time. It had three thousand miles on it, an incredible number of miles for those days. Broke down notwithstanding, Fush, I, and Fisher, the cousin our size, found thrill enough just sitting under the steering wheel and making motor noises with our lips.

And now, the first night out, camped at a lonesome windmill, was proving a gloomy, depressing experience. The plaintive groan of the sucker rods lifting water and the sad cry of kildees around the tank were adding their bit to the mood—a mood I attempted to dispell in talk of happier times.

"Fush, wasn't that some visit though?"

"Yeah."

"And didn't they like us though?"

"Yeah, but..."

"But what?" I asked, astounded not to say distressed that anybody could find any buts about that visit.

"But their greyhounds didn't like old Philip. They sure learnt

39

to treat him with respect, though," Fush said, and promptly went to sleep, worn to a frazzle by romps and runs and prairie dog hunts with the subject he had just broached.

Except for the fact that not far from camp was a spooky motte of mesquite, I'd have joined him. Total recall of that motte was about to bring on the familiar herd of wild apprehensions when, suddenly, I associated old Philip with the situation. A dog that can make a pack of wolf hounds keep their distance could do likewise to a pack of wolves. Or a pack of anything. Yes, old Philip was insurance against the wild animal kingdom just as Papa was against the wild human element, be it in body or in spirit.

"I only wish Papa and old Philip both could be here in bed with me—one on each side," I said to myself. But knowing the natures of each I had to dismiss the wish as just another futile dream. Papa wouldn't sleep in the same bed with old Philip even with me in between them. Neither would old Philip. Which fact hurt me almost as much as if Papa had refused to sleep with me. I never could determine if it was because the old dog just didn't care to sleep with an occasional bed wetter, or if he needed flea-scratching room, fleas being the only creatures alive that seemed to buffalo him. Fact is, the *ruck, ruck, ruck* of his scratching carried to me from the darkness this very minute.

"Dad gum them old fleas. I wish they'd leave old Philip alone." Or did I? With nothing to keep him awake what sort of a watchdog would he make? All of a sudden I found myself in closer kinship with the fleas. They'd see to it that the lobos wouldn't get us. But if old Humpy gets away again we might starve, when the beans and the flour and the potatoes played out. (Here, I didn't mention the sowbelly because I hoped it *would*.) Nope. Old Humpy was still there! I could hear him stomping and chomping out there in the darkness. This association brought on even brighter prospects for a safe journey. Old Humpy, a pure de mustang off the Rio Grande, might not be a bad watchdog himself. Back down there somewhere he must have had a run-in with a panther for he had what appeared a deep claw mark on his hip. Anyhow, when the least thing boogered him at night you could hear him snort a mile off. Probing the remote recesses of my imagination for other fears and finding none, I slipped into slumberland with the others.

Philip and the fleas—not to mention Humpy—having freed me of fears and alarms I joined them and Fush in prairie dog chases next day, and that night beat everyone in camp to dreamland. Too, Sog's sudden—and seldom—silence as regards me and my serenity had lulled me into a false sense of security. It wasn't until the distant skyline of Midland hove into view that the old panics began to push again, panics against which old Philip and the fleas were completely helpless. Just the other day Mama had read us of a child who got lost in a city, never to be heard "hair nor hide of" again. Ever!

But Sog was shortly to set my mind at rest on that score. And replace it with something worse. With the rest of them busy breaking camp he called me aside and in that concerned and confidential manner of his he warned me that we might all smother to death in Midland.

"Ho—how—how's that?"

"Windmills. Hunnerts of 'em. See 'em yonder? So dad gum many, won't be air enough left for us to breathe!"

Windmills losing themselves on the horizon to east and west left me no rebuttal. What's more, had I had one I wouldn't have wasted precious breath on it. Too, such being the case I better leave these prairie dogs go, get back in the wagon. Save what wind I have. It didn't occur to me that the same thing should occur to Fush and old Philip. They kept squandering wind on prairie dogs and jack rabbits. Maybe Sog had windied a little—over-estimated the number of these windmills, but the closer we got the more of these breath-robbers hove into view. Bunches of them, herds of them. And all busy wheeling up precious air!

Here I slammed my eyelids tight shut, to close out the terrifying picture forming in my mind. But it came through clearer than ever. Papa at the Taylor place waiting, waiting, waiting for us to come home. Then searching, searching, searching, but not knowing where to look, thanks to Mama who, for some peculiar reason, had given specific orders that Papa not know where we had gone. Finally, six months, a year, two years, Papa riding up on the rickety remains of a Rock Island wagon, bows splitting, wheels shrunken from their tires, and tattered wagon sheet whipping in the wind. Crumpled here and there would be six bleaching human skeletons, two sets of horse bones, the mummied remains of a dog plus the empty husks of thousands of fleas. But wait. Do fleas breathe? I asked myself, enthralled almost to the point of peace of mind. If they do, it wouldn't be much, so surely there would be enough air for them. But what would they eat with old Philip gone? Nothing, maybe, except the wolves that came to pick old Philip's bones. *And ours!* Tight shut as my eyes were I realized they were leaking like a sieve.

Bawled dry of tears and boiled dry of emotion I began to try to accept this as inevitable, so I may as well find out how soon.

"Wh—when'll we get there?"

"Around dark," Sog surmised, measuring the sun with his hand.

"And we're stayin' all night in the wagon yard. Are we not, Mama?" Blanche asked hopefully—and grammatically—hoping that good grammar would make for a better case.

"Yeah, Mama, ain't we?" Sog asked, his voice too joyful, I figured, for a fellow shortly to face death by suffocation. But this was his nature, and there was nothing I could do to make him face his Maker seriously.

"No we *aren't*," Mama retorted, pronouncing the *aren't* in a way to let us know Sog's *ain't* had been the determining factor. Thank God for bad grammar, I thought, my hopes resurging. Maybe a twelve-hour reprieve, at least.

"No. No wagon yard tonight."

"Why, Mama?" Blanche, of course.

"We're not dressed properly." (Thank God, for once, for rags, I thought.)

"Not even for a wagon yard?"

"Not even for a wagon yard."

"Aw, Mama, where'll we stay then?" from Sog.

"Camp a mile or so this side."

"Yeah, Mama, a mile or so this side," this from me and Fush both. Mine was the tone of voice of a man granted a day's stay of execution, but I was so puzzled at Fush's decision I couldn't help but ask him.

"Ain't no rabbits and prairie dogs in no wagon yard," he said, already a hundred yards from camp, old Philip slobbering at his heels.

This stay, for which I was at first so grateful, now only added to my agony, prolonged the suspense, gave me more time to dwell upon how sweet life was—a steady diet of straight staples notwithstanding, plus faulty-flap bloomer britches and turtle-top straws—and to ponder upon the possibility, the faint possibility of our taking roundants on Midland and maybe escaping such a fate.

A night in the Midland wagon yard with us—from Mama on down to little Gwen and old Philip—smothering and kicking and gasping for air for real couldn't have been more vivid, more horrible than the stark drama being played out in my mind's eye. At least it would be but *once*, over and done with, and not again and again as here in camp.

Characteristic of hope, to spring eternal in the human breast, maybe some way *I* could survive it. Maybe if I took on an extra supply of air tonight I'd pull through. This in mind I began to inhale lungful after lungful of the fresh, dew-sweetened night air, holding each breath until it penetrated every pore. Here I found myself resentful of the traces of campfire smoke that had meant so much to me only the night before. Even so it didn't keep me from inhaling to the very depths of my lungs. I wasn't to know how this procedure would stand me against the morrow; it proved too powerful a sedative for tonight. Shortly I was snoring in the soogans with the rest of them.

Next thing I knew it was an hour by sun and the others were hunkered over their flapjacks, flour gravy and sugar lick. I leapt up squinting into the Midland skyline, hoping that by some miracle —some act of God—the windmills had been removed over night. Not so. There they loomed high and ominous, all over the place, their tails pointing our way as if to say, "Here they come. Prepare to smother." I couldn't help but be a little put out at God. Mama read us where He parted a whole ocean to let the children of Israel pass. And here He couldn't—or wouldn't—knock over a few windmills.

I was just fixing to wheel off and resort to tears when something else on the northern horizon caught my eye—something on beyond and above those windmills—a high, rolling cloud, red and boiling at the top edge. Under ordinary circumstances it would have terrified me, but not today. More like the pillar of fire by night and the pillar of cloud by day that delivered Moses and the children of Israel. This was a big, red sandstorm rolling down from the Staked Plains and it would hit Midland before we did. Consequently, there would be wind enough to go round, even if it did take considerable sand-sifting to breath it. I apologize, God. And I thank thee!

Under ordinary circumstances Midland would have been awesome in its magnitude and frightening for its bustling activity, but much of its awesomeness was lost to me. Partly because of poor visibility but mostly I was too absorbed in the wildly-wheeling windmills. I took a sadistic pleasure in seeing them wheel into the wind like bulls on the prod only to have to turn away with their tails tucked, to escape being wheeled to pieces.

"What you get for tryin' to smother a body," I said.

It was years before I had wit enough to enquire of Sog, "Why didn't the windmills smother them Midland people?"

"Oh, they had enough to go around. It was just when a big bunch, say like us, dropped in unexpected that people smothered."

"Oh," I said, and was right back where I started.

CHAPTER XI

"Is it gonna be sandy like this all the way to Grandma's?" such a whining, whimpering question sounded like me, but it was Fush.

"Yes. And even worse in spots," Mama informed him.

"Then, how many days on in?"

"Four at least, sandy as it is."

"Goleeeeee bummmmm," Fush said, kicking the endgate.

"When the hard land had disappeared so had the prairie dog towns, and with them, Fush's zest. The deep sand had proven too heavy going afoot, even for him. But four days in the wagon was beginning to look like four days in solitary for the likes of him. Result: a mantle of gloom had settled around him. This spirit, or the lack of it, soon pervaded the whole outfit, from old Bullet and Humpy sweating and grunting at the traces back to old Philip, now of sad and sorrowful expression, padding along in the shade of the wagon. The old Rock Island itself seemed to have taken on an air of gloom, moping along in almost complete silence now, as compared to the jolly ring and sing of tires on gravelly roads south of Midland.

I wasn't admitting it, of course, but I was experiencing just the opposite. This was a situation tailor-made for a person of my talents, tastes, and temperament. First, there would be no frightening forecasts from Sog. Second, he couldn't whip up the team and outrun me in this deep sand. Third, this sand was too deep and heavy for a frightening runaway. Fourth, old Humpy would be too petered out to slip his hobbles and sneak away. And even if he did, he could be easily trailed. Fifth, now I wasn't expected to run my fool head off, and tongue out, after prairie dogs. Sixth, I had completely convinced myself that any self-respecting lobo, wild man, or crazy woman would shun this Godforsaken country like a plague. Finally, I had hit upon a method of hypnosis—a means of keeping myself occupied, and preoccupied for hours on end, and without the dangers attendant to lying on the railroad track listening to an approaching train, such as that time on the K. C. M. & O. tracks.

This new discovery was not only safe but simple. All I had to do was keep my chin hooked over the sideboard and my eyes glued on the steady, endless, unchanging rise of the wagon spokes out of the rut, and the steady, endless fall of streamlets of sand from the tire. Mile after mile, hour upon endless hour the rhythmical climb of the spokes and the ceaseless streamlets of sand varied not one jot nor tittle. At least, not to my knowledge. However, it did seem that sometime, somewhere back there an odd-shaped, greasy-black object with a round hole in the middle had flashed, momentarily, onto the roadside. If so it was momentarily, and fleetingly, certainly not enough to stay the steady streamlets of sand and the regular rise of the spokes.

All of a sudden the spokes seemed to abandon their orderly rise and to dodge outward, as if to escape my hypnotic stare. Then there was a violent listing to that side which almost dumped us over the sideboard.

"I didn't aim to do it," I yelled, momentarily obsessed with the idea that I had given it the evil eye. "I mean, I don't know what done it," I said, catching myself. By now, a branding iron on the soles of my feet couldn't have scorched out of me the fact that I saw, in the dim back side of my mind's eye, the axle nut fall into the rut.

47

It took all hands and the cook prying and lifting and straining to get the axle up and the wheel back on. And then it required considerable sifting of sand and searching to find the nut. Although there was fuming in most quarters it was a welcome pause for old Bullet and Humpy, who, as Papa would have put it, were "purt' near played out."

CHAPTER XII

After Uncle Will's out-and-out ranch, lively kids, raunchy greyhounds, and miles of broad open baldies to romp in, Granddad Pollard's sandy land farm was quite a letdown—plowed ground as far as the eye could sweep. Not only that but a yard all littered up with sissy flowers and herbs and blooming shrubs. Not only no place to play but no time to do it, what with all one's strength and energies sapped in toting long-snouted pots to irrigate the place. All of a sudden I felt a longing, a yearning for my own home, or any one of the eight previous ones, with wide-open hard-packed yards. One thing about Papa, and Mama too, for that matter, they didn't clutter up a place with flowers and junk. If they grew anything at all it would be out behind the tank dump. And only then it would be something to eat and not just to look at, say like a row or two of beans or onions or mustard greens (which latter went well with meat grease) or perhaps a couple of tomato vines.

In addition to plowed ground as far as the eye could see and plants crowding out a man's playground, there was that overlong asking the blessing at mealtimes. Whereas we had always pitched right into the sowbelly and sorghum, Granddad waited to thank God for everything, right down to the birds that ate the grasshoppers that ate the crops. Then, for good measure, he would thank God for the grasshoppers for those who might have to fish for their sustenance.

One would think God would get tired of so many thanks and so many pleas and especially of the time it kept Him from more pressing duties. Evidently not, for the Pollard table fairly groaned with good grub—such a variety, in fact, that a selection would have been impossible on a moment's notice. Made a body almost thankful for the long blessings; that way, despite the deeply bowed head, the eye could be busy at selections and rejections.

Fush and I received another near-fatal shock when we learned that Granddad was a preacher—a minister of the gospel, no less. Well, there goes our fun, our excitement, our everything. But, between prayers, Granddad Pollard turned out to be a barrel of fun. Not only that but more exciting to be around than "a couple of dog fights and a horse race," as Sog put it.

Up to now I had hated fiddles and fiddle music. Fiddle music, to me, was fit only as accompaniment to a cat fight, and with the sounds made at a cat fight identical to that of fiddle music, why the music? But Granddad could make a fiddle make music—real music. Better still, he could make a fiddle hoot like an owl, gobble like a turkey, howl like a wolf, nicker like a horse, or bray like a mule. Granddad Pollard could make a fiddle make you a mood—if you wanted to cry he could make you cry, if you needed laughter he could make it make you laugh.

What is more he was a crackerjack yarn spinner to boot. He might put us to sleep with his prayers but he could snap us wide awake with tales of the old frontier. As a button (before his Methodist circuit riding days) he had gone up the trail to Kansas, nearly got a shot at a redskin (until the boss threw his pistol away). And later he trailed a bunch of horse thieves from Buffalo Gap to Coleman town and got his horses back.

There was our other brother, Ralph, and our other sister, Madge. Not as many as the Medlin cousins but just as lively, although they still seemed like an uncle and an aunt. Too, once I had lifted my eyes above the disgusting flowers and shrubs, lo and behold, there stood on the tank dump a giant cottonwood with a swing suspended from its branches. And from the chillingly thrilling height of this swing one could glimpse rangeland out beyond the plowed ground and cattle grazing. And Uncle Fisher, it turned out, added a real western touch by breaking broncs for Granddad and the neighbors. However, Grandma and I didn't see eye to eye as regards the breaking of wild horses. Where I wanted to see one swallow his head and pitch a mile, Grandma lived in horror of one even humping his back. If Uncle Fisher failed to return promptly she would climb the windmill and anxiously scan the sandhills.

"Sog, what makes Grandma so uneasy? Dad gum it. I haven't seen a bronc pitch a lick with him yet," I said, bitterly disappointed at not knowing for certain if he could "ride in a covered wagon" even.

"Grandma has seen him ride. Fact is, she saw a pitching horse turn a cat on him down at the Midland Fair. She lives in dread of him gettin' killed outright one of these days."

"He can ride 'em, then?"

"I should smile, he can ride 'em. Rides 'em all over Texas. Wins big prizes, they say."

Even so, I'd have preferred a little proof positive.

And there was Aunt Embelle who made up for the drab sandy scenery. In my opinion she was beautiful, and I wasn't alone in my opinion, for the place was cluttered with all sorts of suitors ever at her beck and call.

However, all the Pollards, even Granddad, had to play second fiddle to that Pollard food; it topped them all, long blessings notwithstanding. A far, far cry from sowbelly and sorghum, flapjacks and flour gravy. I'd always heard "poor as a parson" but this simply couldn't apply to Granddad. Positively not, for Madge spoke of a cattle deal in which the buyer handed Granddad a check for $2250.00, a sum immeasurable to my fifth-grade brother, much less to me. Consequently I wasn't impressed, until one day the extent of their riches was thrust forcefully upon me by a whole mail-hack load of stuff from Sears & Roebuck—crate after crate from which emanated fascinating aromas.

Shortly, Ralph, armed with claw hammer and pinch bar, laid before our bulging eyes a veritable sesame of marvels—kitchen ware, blankets, farm tools, horse collars, medicines, hair combs, articles of clothing, fiddlestrings, a corset (which made Grandma blush, Mama frown, and Blanche and Embelle snicker, and me impatient for Ralph to get on with it) a buggy wheel, a cobbler's kit, and finally a fancy buggy whip. But by now tears had dimmed the shine of it.

"Why didn't they order *me* somethin'?" I said in a whispering, whimpering aside to Blanche.

"Why, honey, they didn't know you were comin'," Blanche said, putting a comforting arm around me—which didn't comfort. Just as it had helped me assess Granddad's wealth, the shipment brought poignantly home another undefinable feeling—I was homesick. Papa wasn't in this class financially, but he always did manage to bring us some little something. However, before sundown on that same day, so did Granddad—something for everyone of us. But since they hadn't come out of these boxes something seemed amiss. Something *was* amiss with my present—a little red horse hitched to a two-wheeled vehicle. Whoever ever heard of a wagon with just two wheels, unless there had been a bad runaway? And whoever heard of harness with no hames or a belly band and with traces running straight out of the collar? Granddad may have been a mighty good cow trader—$2250 worth—but he sure let some slick toy horse trader skin him here. I could hardly wait to get back and show Papa how poor Granddad got skinned.

In mind and spirit I was already home with Papa but the body was another six or seven days getting back. Papa wasn't there. It seemed like a year but was only a couple of days until he came walking in, his arm in a sling. Since it had to happen I hoped it was a horse falling, a stampede, or something else thrilling. But it turned out he had been kicked while unharnessing the work team.

However, some compensation came from it after all. The sting of Papa's not getting a riding job (and then getting kicked by a common work horse) was lessened somewhat when we learned that of the seven men on the drive, Papa was the only man in the outfit who hadn't got fired or quit before the drive was over. The last ten or twelve days he and the trail boss (a man named Mc-Adoo) had it all to themselves.

"Gollee, Papa," Fush said, admiringly, "You must a seen he—heck amongst the yearlin's then."

"Naw. Gentle as cats. And a nester's pasture to throw 'em in every night. No trouble at all."

"Oh," we said in unison, our enthusiasm dampened to a degree commensurate to a common cook kicked by a common work horse. Doggone Papa. Why couldn't he have embroidered it a little? Granddad could have—and him a preacher.

CHAPTER XIII

January 16, 1914, started off like all the rest of them lately—dull to the extreme, with Papa out hustling for our daily bread, Blanche and Sog in school, Mama reading, little Gwen gumming her thumb, and Fush and I seeking excitement, he by the direct-action method and I via the imagination. Little did we dream that we were soon to kick up excitement enough for Fush himself. Yes, and then some. In fact, excitement enough for all Upland, plus Papa 'way down on the Pecos building fence, and unto our kin folks as far away as Big Spring and Shafter Lake (out of Andrews).

"Hey, Paul. Lookey here!" Lost in the soft dead grass of the tank dump—and a daydream—I didn't take the trouble to look.

"Paul, I said lookey here."

The eye searches last where it least expects to find, so I was a good while locating him. And when the eye did find him it almost popped from its socket.

"Mama, Fush is a-hangin' by his knees from the windmill towerrrrrr!" The thought was father to the word, only the two came out simultaneously. I couldn't determine which startled me the most, his precarious position or his appearance. There he hung, skinny arms spread-eagle, eyes bulging, and long butter-and-molasses hair wilder than usual.

"Fush, you come down from there this minute," I hollered,

simulating Mama's manner of speaking, my panic as genuine as hers would have been under the circumstances.

"Yanhhhhh," he bleated, his hands assuming the position of horns at the head.

"Fush, you come on downnnnnnnnnnnn." By the time I got to the last word I was bawling briskly.

"No rush. Long time till dark."

"Fush. Baawwwwwwww." Just before I'd shifted into the second stages of hysterics he coiled slowly upward like a snake, swung lazily by his hands, groped for the ladder with his feet and came clambering down.

"Paul, you scare me sometimes with them bawlin' spells. I think maybe you've been snake bit."

By guile and other devious means I managed to toll him inside the house (little dreaming I was tolling him out of the frying pan into the fire). Dull and dreary inside, to be sure, but he was less likely to kill his fool self. I don't recall which of us should take the credit; it could have been a mutual inspiration that prompted us to take up from the hearth of the potbellied stove a couple of dead mesquite twigs smoldering at one end, and retire to the shed room.

Hanging there high on a nail was an old coat which furnished us further inspiration. We discovered that by holding these glowing brands beneath the sleeves, smoke would boil out at the collar like the old K. C. M. & O. roaring through the cut east of Rankin. Thrilling! Even so, it wasn't enough to hold Fush's attention for long. His indoor interest span was brief. Soon we were outside looking for more and greater thrills—which weren't long in coming. Shortly we sighted from the top—and bottom—of the windmill a plume of smoke and then a thin tongue of flame licking skyward through the roof of the shed room.

Grabbing up a water bucket and tying an old lariat onto the bail, Fush sent me skedaddling for water from the tank while he shinnied up a back gallery post to the scene of our crime. Scooping up a bucketful I tossed Fush the rope but in reaching for it he lost his balance and fell kerplunk to the ground. Not even allowing himself a second bounce, or the luxury of a groan, he was back on top in a twinkling, pouring water on the flames. I was for calling Mama and darn the consequences. But Fush overruled. Mama was known to panic at the mere wink of a wick. Many was the coal oil lamp or lantern she had banished via the nearest window, just for its sputtering a time or two. Call Mama? Worst thing we could do, he figured, if we had hopes of putting this fire out. Besides, he didn't want any of Mama's excitement, even vicariously. No use fighting fire and Mama both.

"Paul, what you bawlin' for? I'm the one fell off the house," Fush yelled, disgustedly.

"Ain't somebody a-sposed to bawl, at a time like this?"

"Bawl, then, but get a move on with that water."

"Fireeeeeeeeeeeeee!" Mama's cry, louder and more urgent than a locomotive whistle pierced the brisk January air, just as she came hurtling out the back door, little Gwen under one arm and a bureau drawer under the other.

"Fush, Paul, where are youuuuuuu? Oh . . . ."

"Up here, Mama."

"Come-down-here-this-minute! Where's Paul?"

"Around here, Mama!"

"Come-here-this-minute. This-minute!" Mama yelled, her voice carrying more crisp authority than I'd ever heard; so much so that I went immediately. But Fush stood his ground—or, rather, roof.

"We can put it out, Mama. Honest—no wind a-blowin . . ."

Summoning something from somewhere Mama was up the gallery post like a cat and had Fush in hand and back down in a twinkling. Even so, Fush managed another escape or two and a couple of bucketsful hurled from the ground. Inspired by his valor I was likewise able to get in a splash or so, but what with my falling and bawling and dodging Mama, the blaze kept gaining on us. But eventually the fire, plus Mama, made it so hot for us we had to abandon ship.

This time Mama herded us out about a hundred yards, taking a half nelson on each of us to make us stay put. And by this time she'd managed to get a pretty good hold on herself.

"Same old story as when your Papa and I were first married—a burnout. A burnout or a move out. A burnout or a move out that's the Patterson history full turn again."

The roaring, rearing blaze, now spread over half the roof, was licking straight into the windless gray sky. The tinder-dry lumber was beginning to snap and pop and throw out sparks, the latter looking for all the world like our mesquite faggots.

"Purty, ain't it, Fush?" I said, now beginning to get into the spirit of the thing.

"Purty hot," he answered gravely. And in an aside even graver, "But not half as hot as it will be when Papa gets back."

"Oh, Lord. Lordy, I wish somebody would come on," Mama wailed. And immediately, as if the Lord had heard personally, there appeared from the direction of Upland an arrow of dust pointed in our direction, then another, and another.

"That would be the Garners. And the Lanes. And the Millers and Harlans," Fush reasoned soundly, since they now constituted the entire Upland population.

"The Garners and them. My gosh, Fush, me and you don't have no seats in our britches," I said.

"Thought I'd been havin' hot and cold flashes back there," Fush put in. Simultaneously we broke loose from Mama who, simultaneously, let out a terrified, terrifying wail. I pulled up short of the blazing house but Fush plunged on in. Once I got a look at the smoke boiling from the open door I let out a wail fit to put Mama's in the shade. Mama made a move as if to go after Fush but suddenly wheeled and latched onto me, who had no intention of going anywhere.

After what seemed like a whole calendar of days Fush, coughing and gagging, came sprinting out, a bundle under each arm. One was a bundle of clothes the other was a recently acquired picture of Christ.

"Fush, honey, you all right?" Mama screamed, and upon making sure he was, she jarred him loose from his bundles by a terrific box on the jaw.

"Aw, Mama..."

"Mrs. Patterson! Mrs. Patterson?" came a hoarse, anxious voice from the dust cloud. Frantic to present a decent front, Fush and I dived into the bundles and started jerking on our Sunday clothes. Soon we were surrounded by half a dozen, puffing, chattering Garners.

"Youall, all right?"

"Yes, thank God," Mama said.

"Save anything at all?"

"No," Mama said, but she could be excused for lying, what with being in a semihysterical state. We had too saved something. For there at our feet lay the dresser drawer, a blanket, and a battered but still brilliantly-colored Christ under a halo.

"I couldn't just stand there and let God burn up," was Fush's explanation of the latter treasure. But Mama never did reveal why she saved the dresser drawer.

After the excitement had subsided to mere bedlam we discovered an item we could hardly have overlooked, but did. A mattress. Nobody to this day knows how it got there fully a hundred yards from the house. And before we had recovered from this discovery, little Gwen held up something else—her rag doll, the only one who had saved—or rather, rescued—her most prized possession.

Shortly, up clattered three other loads of Uplanders—the remainder of the population except the kids at school. This would be the Lanes, the Millers, and the Harlans, and yonder not far behind, afoot, the Upland student body, led by John Miller (the one who had fallen asleep on guard, but was wide awake now). Then Blanche, her rib stockings sagging, one ribbon of her braid gone and face a-spatter with tears, sobbing and gasping for breath.

"Oh, Lordy, Lord. You—all—all right?"

"Yes, child, yes. All all right."

But to make certain she probed, pinched, and tested each one in turn, little Gwen first, snatching her up with such violence she jarred her loose from the rag doll and a piercing squall simultaneously.

"They tol—told me you—you'd had both legs burnt off."

By now Sog had come huffing in, then J. D. Garner, then Grace Miller, then Ethel Lane, then Edith Lane, then Buster Miller, and so on, while the big Millers and Lanes and Harlans were gathered around asking the same questions as had the Garners. With Blanche here now, Mama was in a position to relinquish responsibility.

"God knows, she's fainted," a coarse male voice hollered, the first clause being a byword, and the second one a fact. After they brought her out of it, which was shortly, I made my way through the milling, yelling, and confusion to Sog, so as to get his reaction to this, the most memorable day of my life.

"Sog, what did it look like—the fire—from out yonder?"

"Well, I'd say it looked like the Pattersons' twenty-fourth move."

"Twenty-third move," Blanche corrected him incorrectly.

In those days western hospitality was a fact and there was considerable quibbling and squabbling over who would have the honor and the privilege of taking us in until we could get established in *twenty-five*. Since there were close to a dozen Millers, many of whom had already left home, we wound up at their house.

CHAPTER XIV

Breakfast over, the Miller boys set up a howl to hike out and explore the ruins—to poke and probe into the dying embers of Mama's hopes and dreams of a permanent home, the end of the wagon tracks.

"Purty please, Mama," Dick rumbled, having to look 'way down to anticipate his Mama's answer.

"All right, then," she said, wheeling to bore a stern eye into John. "But watch over Dick and them. Hear?"

"Yes, ma'am."

"OK with you, Mama?" Sog asked.

"I suppose so."

We left there running.

"Paul, you can't go," Sog said, "you're too little."

"Don't care. I'm still a-goin'."

"Won't be no dinner."

"Don't care. I'm still a'goin'."

"It's three miles out there and six back," Sog said, stretching it both ways to discourage me.

"Don't care. I'm still a-goin'."

"All right. But don't come a bawlin' around to me when you give out. And get hungry."

The expedition of eight, counting old Philip and the Miller dog,

Bowser, must have covered five miles in the process of gaining the first one, what with chasing chaparral birds, prairie dogs, and one another. I was duly grateful when Captain John set a southeasterly course and held strictly to it. Even so, I was hard put to keep the whine out of my voice and the growl out of my stomach long before we reached our destination.

Momentarily, my weariness and hunger were dispersed in the eager exploration of the charred ruins. But a green glob of melted windowpane, the charred skeleton of Papa's old .45 pistol, and the blackened remains of Sog's .22 rifle were no substitute for food and rest.

"Sog."

"Yeah."

"I'm hungry."

"Don't tell me. I ain't a apple," Sog cracked, bringing a laugh from everybody else.

"I *am* hungry."

"Here, then. Have a slice of baked ham." He pitched me the warped, blackened remains of our iron piggy bank, which article I disdainfully spurned. Buster picked it up and shook it. "Why, Paul, it's got money in it."

"Don't care if it's got a hundred dollars in it. Sog."

"Yeah?"

"I'm tired."

"Pore little feller, 'course you are. Here, lay down for a spell."

He shoved me toward the collapsed, twisted remains of an iron bedstead, which act tickled Fush and the Millers half to death but left me cold—not to say tired and hungry.

A foray through the barn yielded an abundance of cow and horse feed—cottonseed cake, oats, corn, alfalfa, all of which was manna from heaven to me. And I couldn't help but notice that the others, with the exception of old Bowser, were chomping away with a right good will. Old Philip had learned to eat anything we could—which was anything.

Pockets bulging with barnyard provisions and arms burdened with plunder the already weary expedition was plodding homeward. Long gone was the hilarity, the front-and-rear scoutings, the side excursions, the horse play. Just tramp, tramp, tramp across the endless plain. Then over hill and down dale, only to be confronted by another hill higher and dale deeper. Like immigrants on the old Oregon Trail, our wake was strewn with abandoned equipment. A burnt .45 skeleton here, a scorched .22 barrel there, a pitiful pile of cottonseed cake over yonder, scatterings of corn kernels back there, and so on. Surely, the world's longest, most gruelling two miles.

"Sog."

"I'm hunnnnngry," Sog said, beating me to it, which fact made me rock-throwing mad. But I must conserve my strength.

"Sog."

"I'm tirrrred."

What sent a homicidal urge through me this time wasn't so much what he said, but the fact that he'd jumped up and cracked his heels together. However, I noted with a twinge of satisfaction that he'd had to rid himself of considerable plunder.

"Wisht Dick would get shed of that old junk," I whimpered, inwardly, visions of a piggyback ride swimming in my head. Or was it just my poor head swimming? Oh, how could a child's feet be so heavy and his stomach so light. The stock feed hadn't proven out so sustaining or satisfying. No wonder old Humpy was always trying to slip off.

The next ballast I dumped was a generous portion of salt, washed out and overboard by tears. Dimly, through the damp of my eyes I saw Dick, up ahead, transfer his booty to John. I broke into a lumbering run. Then I saw, through redampening eyes, that half-grown Buster jump aboard Dick's back and ride off like he owned the JMs. Head bowed by weary miles—and now by hopelessness— I trudged wearily on, eyes downcast and spirits likewise.

"Dad gum Sog. He could carry me if Dick could Buster. Either

that or he could of made me stay home. Bawww. Awwwwuhhhh."
Bowed head lower now and one leaden foot dragged wearily in
front of the other, I resigned myself to death by creeping exhaus-
tion and galloping hunger. I had just reached the bottom of a seemingly bottomless vale without sufficient strength, I figured, to take
a 10 per cent incline. All of a sudden my head was wrenched
around by the thunder of hoofs. Hard on the fleeing heels of Philip
and Bowser came a herd of wild mules.

"JM mules after us," I squalled, taking that 10 per cent incline
as if it were down hill.

"Wild mules after us!" the cry rang out all up the line.

The gravity of the situation hit me even harder when I passed
Fush. For the first time in his life he was running *from* something.
And running earnestly, his face screwed up by something besides
mischief. Buster, big, fat squab, had jumped loose from Dick and
was bounding on ahead like an antelope, though Dick was showing
a powerful stride himself. Sog had glanced back as if to give me a
leg up. A thoughtful but useless gesture. About that time I shot by
him like he was staked to a tree.

John had long since jettisoned his booty and was being over-
hauled by the entire expedition. But he wasn't exactly asleep like
he was on guard that time. Then I realized that he was acting as a
sort of rear guard, minding his mother to look out for us.

"Lord, don't Thou let them mules lay a hand on us, but if they
get pore John, forgive him for going to sleep on guard that
time . . . ," I prayed, comforted in the fact, and doubly thankful,
that a man didn't have to stop and kneel down to pray. Had that
been the case "pore John" would have been without my petition.

The town section fence, and safety, was looming ever nearer
now, but the thunderous hoofbeats were sounding ever louder. My
overtaking seven-eighths of the expedition was small comfort to a
child of my imagination. Whereas a dying man's past flashes before
him, the future was being projected in front of my eyes: little Paul
didn't make it. His body lying out there in the JM mule pasture,

pawed and chawed to a bloody pulp (like the wild mules did the little boy in Arizona Territory years ago). Everybody bent over him, crying. Papa, Mama, Blanche, and so on down. Even old Philip, howling his head off.

"He was such a brave little thing," Blanche would be saying.

"He done it to save us," Sog would be telling them. "Held back a-purpose. So's the rest could get away. While—while they was a chawin' on him."

Then Papa would take up Sog's story and pass it on, even though Papa was no hand at all to brag, and most especially no hand to lie. He just thought so much of me.

I fought down the temptation to turn my head and let my eye behold what my mind's eye had already confirmed—death at the hands of gnawing teeth and pawing hooves.

"Yawheeeeeee, yawheeeee." The bray and hot breath of a mule, obviously, sent a new surge of power through my legs. Buster was the first one under the wire, his squabby body twanging the bottom strand like the string of a steel guitar. Old Philip and I were a photo second, with old Philip's tail actually a little farther back than mine, with Sog, Dick, and Bowser finishing in that order. John, a poor eighth, considered himself God-blessed in getting under the fence at all, what with missing a chawing by the skin of a mule's teeth. It was revealed later that the lead mule had actually gotten a nip at John as he went plummeting under the wire.

"Where'd he nip you, John?" Sog asked.

"Where else could a mule bite a man bringin' up the rear?"

Braced, refreshed, rejuvenated by our deliverance, home seemed only a hop away.

"Papa's here." Fush said, not quickening his pace any. At these words my heart and feet turned back to lead, and I began to wonder how much must a child go through with in one day. Yet there was more. The moment of facing Papa was here, and it wouldn't or couldn't be other than the moment of *truth*.

"Your Mammy don't know what started the fire. Do you?"

Papa had put the question between us. This was one of those rare occasions when I didn't have anything to say. It wasn't necessary; Papa had an eye that could probe into the remotest recesses of the brain and heart.

"Spit it out." Papa said, now enlightened except for a few minor details.

"Well," Fush's voice came as from afar, "we was playin' choo choo train in the back room." He addressed a small stone on the ground and then kicked it as if offended by its presence.

"We was usin' little bitty fires on little bitty old mesquite twigs," I put in hopefully, as if it would lessen the punishment of the crime.

"I'm startin' a little bitty fire myself," Papa said. "You fellers step here behind the tank dump."

I was thankful, however, for one thing, thankful that Papa hadn't gotten hold of us before Fush made that last dash into the burning house for overalls with seats in them!

CHAPTER XV

Because of wardrobe difficulties our early school days were wretched to say the least. We never could get our ensembles to come out even. When we got new pants our heels were showing. And by the time we got new stockings, vice versa. A Rankin boy by the name of Atwood King showed us a handy household hint on how to disguise an unsightly heel hole that appeared above the shoe top—paint the naked hide with shoe polish. But shoe polish ever in short supply, we merely folded the sock foot under and walked higher on the sock. Mrs. Ham, our teacher, though a kind, understanding woman, used to say I sometimes reminded her of Hamlet during one of his insane spells. "Hose, fouled, ungartered, and down-gyvved, . . ." I didn't know who this Hamlet was or what ran him crazy but I had an idea it was rubber inner tube garters, which in our case came in two sizes—one that would hold up your stockings (and cut off the circulation) and the other size you would have to wear on the thighs with safety pins suspended on strings to hook in the tops. This latter we shunned like a rattle-snake—looked too much like women's hose supporters. Switching, swapping out with each other was no solution either. Invariably we both drew garters that would hold one stocking up and let the other drop, hence, switching didn't help, except it alternated circulation in the legs, giving each one time about.

Summing up—mine and Fush's wardrobe difficulties were Sog's wardrobe difficulties *made over*. That is, in case Aunt Embelle happened to come down and make them over. Otherwise, we had to wear Sog's castaways anyhow, made over or not. Or make do with what we had until we could afford more, which was usually, as Papa put it, "a right smart while."

Scholastically, the situation wasn't much better. Fush spent all summer teaching me the first page of "Playmate's Primer," said page consisting of four terse sentences:

> "This is Will."
> "How do you do, Will?"
> "This is May?"
> "How do you do, May?"

I was happy enough to meet May, although she wasn't in Sis' or Mable's class. But rapport with Will was instant. Well, not so much rapport as sympathy and pity. The poor little feller had on a turtle-topped straw exactly like mine, complete down to the home-made twine-string throat latch. (I think this is why Fush had such a bitter aversion to book-reading for so many years.)

Page 1 of "Playmates" stowed snugly in memory I was a big success that first day of school. But Mrs. Ham's hopes of having a prodigy on her hands were blasted sky winding when I spent the next thirty days or so on page two. A "reading block" is the modern polite term, when a "block head" might apply, as it did in my case.

The wooden schoolhouse, situated on the side of a gentle hill on the Upland–JM road, consisted of two big rooms, only one of which was still in use. In the other was stored the wreckage of past years—broken two-seater desks the marble sharks had scuttled for the ball bearings. These steel bearings made first class taws, but were murder to glassies and crockies when in the hands of specialists like Dick Miller. The classroom furnishings consisted of the American Flag, a picture of George Washington, a picture of a big ship in full sail on a stormy sea, two green blackboards, Mrs. Ham's desk, a potbellied stove, and a dozen two-passenger desks upon whose tops were carved the entire history of Upton County romance.

Deeply-carved heart outlines entwined such names as Arthur & Grace, Chunky & Oscar, Lancelot and Bessie, Velma and Percy, Ethel and Jack. However, the fact that these desks were so labeled by no means meant that students were seated in this manner—the boys sat on one side of the room and the girls sat on the other side. These names were carved by the boys at snatches of odd intervals behind the risky, and uncertain privacy of a propped up "joggafy" book (this being the largest book of that day).

As soon as I could read these names, I could also read between the lines as to which was true love, which was a mere companionship of convenience, and which Romeo loved self more than others.

For example "Arthur and Grace" meant that this was merely an alliance of convenience. Or it could mean that Arthur really loved Grace but was also a hopeless, helpless egomaniac. "Lancelot and Bessie" could have meant the same thing as "Arthur and Grace" which was certainly not very knightly of him, whatever the alliance. Percy, of course, truly loved Velma, as was the case with Jack and Ethel. But the one who drew my complete admiration—and Fush's—was the loner of the bunch, the free man, the unfettered Russell Bell. The name in bold, deep strokes was carved square in the middle of a two-passenger desk.

The student body consisted of some eight or ten students—the little ones of the Millers, Lanes, Garners, and Pattersons, Wanda Harlan, and sporadically, not to say spasmodically, Bill and Pat Collins. For extras there was Jack and Bill Mayfield occasionally, and Mrs. Ham's boy, Claud. Since grades went only as high as the sixth or seventh, Dick Miller and Jack Mayfield were the only big kids left in school. John, Grace, Blanche, Sog, and all the bigger Garners, Lanes, Millers, and Harlans had already obtained their educations and moved out into the working world (except some of the girls who had gone to more advanced schools elsewhere). In fact, Sog, now fourteen, had already launched forth into his chosen career. He was drawing a grown cowboy's wages down at the JM.

The retentiveness of my memory harbors only those things that shouldn't have taken place. On April Fool's day, true to an old tradition, we invariably sneaked off to a windmill in the JM beef pasture and spent the shank of the day engaged in gourd battles. Most dirt tanks were covered with a tangle of gourd vines, and the gourds (ranging from lemon to apple size) made better grenades than cow chips. Far more lethal, unless deterioration had set in. I always chose the deteriorated ones, not from the humane standpoint but for fear of retaliation in kind. Fush, Bill Collins, and some of the others, however, stuck with the deadly variety, just as in the cow chip fights.

Then there was the time Jack Mayfield heated a tap on the top of the stove and dropped it down the back of Claud Ham's collar. For a chubby boy Claud handled himself with astounding agility, jumping back and forth over desks with his mother in hot pursuit. All the while he was fighting at his back and letting out blood-clabbering shrieks. With the aid of Dick and four little boys strong for their ages, Mrs. Ham finally got Claud down and discovered what made him kick. Jack Mayfield was quickly apprehended, taken to the junk room and soundly razor-stropped. However, from the appearance of the two I couldn't tell who had stropped whom. Jack reentered unruffled and smiling but poor Mrs. Ham came back on the ragged edge of the shouts. She strode over and sighted down Claud's backbone again. "Jack Mayfield, you have branded this child for life!"

"Well, then," Jack drawled, "he's mine from now on. He's got my brand on him."

I would have given a pair of little boy's shop-made cowboy boots for that much nerve. I expected Mrs. Ham to half kill Jack now, but she just let out books and led Claud (still flinching and faunching) into their living quarters, which was a curtained-off portion of the junk and store room.

CHAPTER XVI

Our case of wanderlust cured—or at least arrested—Fush and I vowed we would never willingly move away from dear old Upland. How it shocked and saddened us to discover that the opposite was occurring under our very eyes. Upland was moving away from us, with Papa helping it move house by house. Rankin had lured the Garners and then the Millers. Sis out of my life forever. Irreplaceable—until Mabel Lane stepped in. Up to now I had carefully avoided Mabel because of the psyche-shattering question she had asked me before we were formally introduced: "Do you wet the bed?" Which question I had answered falsely.

"I do," she confessed, "and Mama whips me."

Whereas Sis would snatch up and inspect bugs, beetles, lizards, grasshoppers, frogs, and even mice, Mabel would jump behind me and scream. But shortly Mabel was snatched from my protective custody when the Lanes were lured to Rankin.

Upland life turned dull and lonesome now that we constituted the entire boy population. Still lots of social activity, however, for the grown folks. The courthouse was still the setting for dances and midnight suppers. On these occasions the hitch racks would fill with buggy and saddle stock, the courtroom with dancers and the jury room with sleeping kids (each tagged and labeled against baby-switching pranksters). Many of the menfolks would fill up with whiskey but went ahead and conducted themselves like gentlemen.

What wonderful, delicious midnight suppers. But what a bitter struggle to stay awake until they hollered "chuck." The interminable *thrunk thrunk squeeeeekkkk squeeeeekkkk* of the fiddle tuning was a trial and ordeal, with the music itself not much better. Especially to one who had heard Grandpa Pollard fiddle. Once the dancing started it practically drowned out the fiddling. Thereafter they kept time keeping an eye on each other's elbows and feet.

At that time there must have been around a hundred grown people in Upton County and outlying areas, all present and accounted for at the dances, of course. The percentage must have run about 75–25, men 3 to 1 over women. (It didn't occur to me to wonder whether the other 50 women were the ones crouching in nesters' rafters for miles around). These women, being so outnumbered, had to have exactly three times the endurance of the men.

With one or two exceptions these socials went off in a very orderly and circumspect manner. One night, however, there was an attempt at gunplay between two cowboys (whose names will have to remain anonymous for security reasons) over the attentions of beautiful Velma (or, perhaps, Chunky) Garner. Cowboy B wasn't making any headway. A sharp argument arose between the rivals and B decided to make up in valor what he lacked in charm. He invited Cowboy A outside. B, never a snappy dresser at best, usually belted up his trousers hurriedly and without benefit of belt loops. This bit of negligence not only brought about his social and romantic downfall but the downfall of his trousers as well. Halfway to the door the idea struck B that perhaps it would better impress the girl if he outpistoled his rival right here in her presence. Suddenly he crouched, fished beneath his shirt and withdrew a mammoth .45. Since he wasn't much bigger around than this six shooter the slack in his belt was too much. *Swoop.* Down went his pants. Like a hawk diving for a chicken, B went down after them and came up running for the door. Cowboy A, his triumphant rival, added insult to humiliation by yelling at the fleeing B. "Next time you better wear yore spurs."

Another time Sog got hold of some strange stuff in the jury room. Result: he almost turned over the supper table, stepped in the face of a guitar and fell downstairs square on top of me. However, he is not to be too sorely censured for such uncharacteristic conduct. He had on a brand spanking new Sears & Roebuck suit with his first long pants, plus a pair of shop-made boots bought with his own wages. Who wouldn't feel his oats—or rye—under the same set of circumstances? Besides, the measures Papa would take once he got wind of it would be censure enough.

The latest and greatest craze in ballroom dancing was the turkey trot. "Everybody's doing it, doing what? The turkey trot!" so said a song of the same name. Well, not everybody. Among the staid and the stable it was a work of the devil—not really a turkey trot but a high lope to hell, spawned by the same, evil, insidious influence that had caused once-respectable girls to bob their hair and buff their fingernails.

"My daughter do the turkey trot? Definitely not."

My utter fascination with cowboys notwithstanding, I always found my mind's eye coming back to the suppers they would eventually spread—"fancies" for the most part: salads of all sorts, cakes of all makes, vegetables of every variety, sauces of assorted flavors, tea with actual chunks of ice floating in it, coffee to appeal to the most eccentric of caffein addicts—the works. These visions of sugarplums dancing in my head always brought out that old aversion to fiddles (Granddad Pollard, excepted) knowing that their wailings were all that stood between me and this feast. And it would be these fiddles that would continue to apply double torture to me for the next three hours, to prolong my internal yearnings until midnight. With every dragging moment I could see more clearly why Sog was forced to that move in the jury room. How could any sane or sober man stand this delay?

Papa attended these shindigs when he had time which was seldom. Though he enjoyed the visiting and the vittles he never was known to dance a step. Not that he opposed dancing, at least on religious grounds. Probably just didn't have the heart to get out there and tromp on those pounds and pounds of perfectly good corn meal they strewed around to make the floor slicker. To come right down to it, the only steps Papa believed in taking were to and from work.

Mama never attended these affairs with or without Papa. She would, however, attend the protracted meetings and brush arbor revivals with or without Papa. Generally, it was without Papa. Papa, though a man of few vices, steered shy of protracted meetings, brush arbor revivals, and circuit riders as much as possible. Perhaps, like most old time cowboys he was salvation shy. Or most likely it was like Sog says, "Papa's afraid they might spring that old gospel hymn on him—"I Shall Not Be Moved." For an old itch-footer like Papa, with at least two dozen moves behind him and another one contemplated, this would be too much." Both Papa and Mama would attend the Friday evening concerts in the schoolhouse occasionally, to hear the elocution students declaim.

CHAPTER XVII

The hustle and the bustle of city life, the surge and urge of exciting Upland has so enthralled us, so occupied our time and attention up to now, that we have clean overlooked a couple of moves—*twenty-five* and *twenty-six*.

Move *twenty-five* from the shack on the square to the Finley place a mile east of town was a joy, a comfort, and most especially a relief to Mama. It was a joy because of the greater living space, a comfort because it wasn't so accessible to visitors and mere passers-by asking road directions, hence a quieter environment in which to read and correspond. It was a relief because it furnished far fewer hazards to life and limb—not hers, but ours. No courthouse roof to slide down, no high attic to fall out of, no tall windmill to cut monkeyshines on, no city water to pollute or drown in while swimming, no tall wooden fences to seesaw on. Those long joints of cast off four-inch pipe we had to use for seesaws had a tendency to roll out from under us—hence frequent contusions, lacerations, and abrasions.

Consequently, the Finley place wasn't so frightening as downtown Upland either by day or by night. Practically no place here that Fush could get himself (and/or me) killed by day and fewer frightening sounds by night.

Twenty-five met with Blanche's complete approval also. And she was duly appreciative of Papa's stepping beyond his means to make her happy. This involved a 100 per cent increase in rent. Now it was $3.00 per month as compared to the shack's $1.50. It was a bigger, nicer house with actual wall paper on some of the walls. Mainly it afforded Blanche more privacy.

To Papa and Sog, *twenty-five* was just another move, didn't matter one way or the other since they were seldom at home anyhow; but to Fush, it was a terrific shock, a terrible letdown, a gross betrayal. What to do to kill the monotony? No courthouse roof to slide down, no tall windmills to cut monkeyshines on, no high attics to fall out of, no city water to pollute, no pipe seesaws to roll out from under one. No nothing. What's more, the varmints here at *twenty-five* were no more plentiful than right there in Upland, "which ain't fair to us and old Philip."

Fush and the old dog remedied the situation by taking to going with Papa on freighting and fencing trips. As for me, I could always lapse back into dreamland, which I did. The only wild, exciting, incredible thing to happen to me—outside my vivid imaginings—was the time I rescued our four blue brindle kittens from the aftermath of a sudden shower. But too late. When I lifted them from the mud and slush of their bed in the barn they showed not the faintest spark of life. Nothing left to do but dig them a common grave in the greasewoods. However, when it came to shoveling that gooey stuff back over them, I didn't have the heart. Sorrowfully, I made my way back to the house leaving, literally, a trail of tears behind me.

The morning sun was just now clearing the greasewoods to the east, the beginning of a long, long day. At least there would be sunshine after last night's rain. But what difference would sunshine make on such a sad, sad day? It made all the difference in the world! It revived all nine lives of all four cats and they were back big as life and twice as lively by nine o'clock that morning. Regardless of what happens to Fush on the Pecos he can't top this. Of this I was so certain I met the Rock Island wagon a mile from the

Finley place just to see if he could top it. For once and for a wonder he couldn't.

Move *twenty-six* (or was it *twenty-seven?*) which was to come shortly was to the Gaines place, just a dull duplication of the Finley place only more so. Moving now was just a matter of cheaper rent, since there was still work enough in the vicinity. The only stirring event to occur at the Gaines place was Papa's announcement that we were moving into the Upland jail, residence part. Papa was to work part time in the sheriff's office, act as jailer and we would feed the prisoners on a contract basis so much per meal.

Of all our moves from "pillar to post," as Mama so often put it, this number *twenty-seven* (or *twenty-eight*) proved to be the "pillar" in one sense of the word. It was the most rewarding of all from the standpoint of both finance and recreation. Foremost, it put me and Fush back on that courthouse roof, back on and in the city water, back on the rolling seesaws and back on the windmill. And almost as interesting were the occasional guests we received there at the jail—most especially upstairs in the cells.

Too, the flat, asphalt-gravel roof yielded excellent chewing gum in season. By night it afforded a splendid observatory from which to study the constellations, and from which Fush could jump down onto the kitchen roof some eight to ten feet lower.

In addition to that, the jail afforded us our very first experience with indoor toilet and running water, thus sparing us from those long, onerous water hauls by day and those long, frightful bathroom runs by night. But behind every compensation there lurks a drawback. In this bathroom with its lavatory and indoor john sat a bathtub and in this bathtub sat Fush and Paul far too frequently, when Blanche was around. Not at first, but just as soon as the novelty wore off, however, we learned that by filling the tub to the brim—to where we could almost swim in it—baths could be fun but tended to loosen the wall plaster and attract centipedes in droves.

Best of all the county of Upton furnished coal to burn thus eliminating the blister-busting, callous-raising chore of cutting down and hauling in, cutting up and carrying in mesquite wood for kitchen and living room. Rustling kindling was bad enough. Finally, the fact that Patterson finances were improved deserves a chapter by itself, which shall appear later.

CHAPTER XVIII

"Paul, 'cept for me and you and Mama and them, this would be a ghost town," Fush pointed out.

"You mean ghosts would take over if we was to move out?" I asked, my spinal column sharing equal billing with the horror and prideful emotions racing from my brain. Horrified at the thought of a courthouse and jail full of ghosts and yet thrilled to think that a cowardly creature like me was partly responsible for keeping them scared off. Mama and I were the scary ones, but neither would sympathize with or tolerate this weakness in the other. I couldn't understand such a weakness in Mama what with no big brothers around to jump out of hiding at her, spin her blood-curdling stories, or hoodwink her into hazardous adventures.

On the other hand, Mama couldn't conceive of how I would consistently fall for such farfetched fantasies as Sog and Fush fed me—crazy women in the rafters, wild men, half headless ones in pastures. She wasn't so easily boogered by day, but come dark she would spot more spooks than a raw bronc and I could uncover in broad day. What's more, her boogers were wired for sound—voices, such as drove us out of the Taylor place that time on a visit to Grandma Pollard.

Mama, then, was as panic prone as I, in fact, more so. For in those long night vigils, overcome eventually by drowsiness, I would drop off to sleep. Not Mama. She had been known to keep an all night watch on a suspicious, man-like shape in a mulberry tree, which the light of day would reveal as a tow sack.

Many was the night she would have cried "wolf" but for fear of bringing the wolf down to devour us in our beds. Cry wolf often and earnestly enough and one day it is likely to appear. Such was the case on at least two occasions here at the halfway ghost town of Upland. Toward dark one summer evening something had boogered us out of our quarters in the jail and we were huddled, Mama, Fush, Gwen, and I, on the west stile leading over the courthouse fence to the old abandoned post office. It was a typical Edgar Allen Poe type of evening with beetling-black, lightning-laced rain clouds boiling overhead and an eerie wind moaning through the mulberries.

We were huddled there wondering whether to risk the spooky old post office as a refuge from the storm when a vivid flash of lightning outlined on the courthouse's upstairs front gallery the figure of a man. He was leaning out and looking down as if anticipating the exit of someone from the opening underneath. He wore a wide-brimmed gray hat, a blue shirt, and heavy tan ducking britches of a type popular with cowboys of that day. Darkness. Then another flash of lightning. This time he was gone. Strangely enough, not a single word from any of us, from Mama on down. Stranger still was the fact that so fearful, and so garrulous a child as myself would keep silent. Perhaps I dismissed it as the figment of an overwrought imagination, since the courthouse gallery wall was at least waist-high. And this being the case, how could I have seen the yellow ducking britches? Most incredible of all how could I have kept this secret for nearly fifty years? But I did. When I had outlived, and partially outgrown, the reputation of an overly active imagination, I broached the subject to Fush. He had seen him too, yellow britches and all. And he too had kept it to himself for all these years, partly, I expect, from fear of developing a reputation like mine.

But not long thereafter something or somebody definitely not a figment of the imagination paid us a visit in the middle hours of the night. We had bolted the back entrance to the jail, and shoved against the front door a table loaded with staples—potatoes, flour, beans. With no little bitterness on my part—dad gum me and Fush —great hands to take off and lose locks and doorknobs. Why weren't we just as good at putting them back on?

Mama and Gwen had taken to bed leaving Fush and me to our pallet on the floor. Mama's keen ear was the first to pick it up—a faint scuffing of gravel in the front yard. Dad gum old Philip, just like him to be off with Papa when we needed him. And, come to think of it, dad gum Papa too!

"Fush, I—I wisht me and you hadn't . . . " my reaching hand stopped me in midsentence. Fush wasn't there. Neither was his answer forthcoming. "Oh, Lord, even Fush has run out on us . . ."

I was fixing to let out a piercing squall when my groping hand felt him. Not only him but the cold, slick barrel of Papa's .30-.30 Winchester pointed in the direction of the door. About this time there was a definite testing of the door, a pressing against it. Then another one. Stronger. A pause. An interminable space of apprehension, and then the sound of receding footsteps. What changed the night prowler's mind? Was it a premonition? Or was it the actual sound of a .30 shell being thrown into the chamber of a rifle by a kid only nine years old and as skinny as a rifle barrel, but with a pretty steady bead on the door and a mighty touchy finger on the trigger?

CHAPTER XIX

I envied the Reeds, our new—and only—neighbors, their Buick, deactivated though it might be. But I was likewise proud of Papa's progress from unemployed cow inspector to cowman in three short years, from seventy-five cents to a herd of cattle between 1913 and 1916. He had bought seven head of scrub cows from John R., for which he was paying with the steer end of the calf crop. What's more, two mares, a horse called Polecat, and a white jenny burro now bore the XE Bar brand.

Although legally ours, some ten or twelve Dominecker chickens bore no man's brand (except for a couple of the oldest and slowest ones with Fush's and my green paint XE Bar). Since they got nothing from us, except what little corn they could snitch from the trough when the horses were fed, why should they lay us eggs? And since they were forced to run with the road runners and compete with them for grasshoppers and lizards, why not just lay their eggs with the road runners? Gathering the eggs was just one long Easter egg hunt, and, but for Fush, a fair-to-middling naturalist by now, no telling what our breakfast egg menu would have read —road runner, owl, buzzard, crow, or Dominecker.

Success breeds success. Prosperity begets affluence. While our cold-blooded cattle were dropping a calf or two every year or so, Papa was having success in politics. Now, he was county treasurer, knocking down a salary of $300 per year. He was also serving as sheriff's office deputy at a dollar a day, this plus the freighting and fencing contracts on the side. And there was the prisoner-feeding contract at so much per meal, and our living quarters in the jail were rent free. As I or any other fool could plainly see, move *twenty-seven* or *twenty-eight* was wise. It had brought Papa closer than ever before to living within his means (though the "fancies" showed no appreciable increase in our pantry).

Although Mama was overjoyed and astounded with the running water, the kitchen sink, the bathroom bathtub, bath water and indoor "closet" all in the same arrangement, she soon grew weary, not to say bitter, over the prisoner-feeding arrangement. "I don't feel like cooking for my own family. Much less prisoners," Mama said, "and especially that surly scoundrel you have up there now."

"But, wife . . ." That is as far as Papa's rebuttal went. We could tell he was trying to get along this time by his saying "wife" instead of "old woman." Possibly because he realized Mama never did feel really well, and because he agreed with her on the guest upstairs—a hard *hombre* of Old Mexico antecedents, in for knifing an *amigo* turned *enemigo*. The feeling was mutual. He didn't like Mama's cooking either. Cornbread, molasses, sowbelly and black coffee. He thought he was getting "short-potted" on his grub.

"Me no hoss. Me no eat corn," he said.

"What's *bueno* enough for wife and little *muchachos* ought to be *bueno* enough for you," Papa said, and he wasn't trying to be sassy. Nor was he trying to appear learned; he was merely throwing in all the Spanish he knew to try to make the fellow understand.

Most of our upstairs guests were of Mexican origin. Not that they were meaner than Anglos, it was just that they lacked influence, affluence, pull, political affiliations. Though Anglos might crack one another over the head with pistols, knock each other down and out with breastyokes, get drunk and disorderly, steal an occasional horse or cow, or even gun somebody down, for them there was always available bail or bond and influence with juries.

Very rarely did we ever have more than one upstairs guest at a time, but one night, while the unpleasant one was still up there, Mr. Garner showed up with another prisoner. The sheriff's new prisoner, a big cowboy, was obviously jealous of his freedom not to say plumb terrified of being fenced in. Consequently he broke loose, cleared the wooden fence in one jump and disappeared into the darkness.

Cowboys were notoriously poor travelers afoot but this one beat Mr. Garner's new Buick back to Rankin, his starting incentive being a couple of .45 slugs Mr. Garner sent singing above his head, just to remind him he was dallying with the law. Ordinarily, Fush and I would have been honored with this cowboy's company. Or even pleased that he had made his getaway, but a slur he let fall just before he broke loose ripped his California britches with us.

"I druther spend a night in *hell*," he yelled.

"*Pos, hombre* whare theenk you, you at now, hey?" came the voice of our upstairs guest. The Mexican's crack made Fush just as mad and me too, when I caught the drift of it, but the Mexican was out and long gone by then.

Mexican sheepherders were our most frequent guests—those who had supposedly gone *loco* from lonesome. Herders in their right mind were low enough in the esteem of society as a whole—much less the poor demented ones. But Fush and I found these herders, without exception, among the finest people we ever met. Our favorite upstairs guest was a little old herder named Pedro something—Pedro Martínez, quite likely, since Martínez seems to be the Mexican equivalent of Smith.

Pedro was jailed simply because of a premature prediction as to the end of the world. He had eaten his chickens, turned his burro out, given away his household goods, attired himself in his night shirt, confessed his sins, and retired to the top of the Rankin stockpens hill to await Judgment Day, which was due, he predicted, the coming Thursday.

Came Thursday but not the full Judgment, only that of poor

Pedro, whom they slapped in jail. In our estimation this was the biggest miscarriage of justice since Nero had Christians thrown to the lions. But we were mighty happy that Pedro was with us. It wasn't three days until Don Pedro had our support for any office of any land, U. S., Mexico, or wherever. Kind, congenial, comical, patient, and the finest harmonica player ever to come down the line was Pedro. When he tucked that French harp out of sight under that big black *mustacio* and sighed into it *canciones de muerte y amor* (songs of death and love) even Fush would hold still for hours on end.

"Peedrow, play 'Sack I Take Us'," we'd say, our gringo accent so thick we may as well have asked for "Turkey in the Straw." But Pedro, somewhat of a specialist on accents, would encore *Zacatecas* until the world looked level and life smooth.

Typical of the race (and of the profession) Pedro had a heart as big as all outdoors and as soft as a lamb's fleece. He couldn't rest easy until he had forced upon us his money and his watch. The money we had no place to spend—no use for, and so forced it right back. But we found his watch highly tinkerable. When he called for his knife (which was purposely left on a shelf downstairs), our heart was as generous as his. Unhesitatingly and unquestioningly we ran down and fetched it. Next he asked for a soft pine box which we likewise produced.

Out of this, plus a few other odds and ends, he whittled us an exact replica of a windmill, assembling it outside the bars in hours upon hours of tedious, painstaking work. The finest, most fascinating present we had ever received, so fascinating, in fact, that I, as well as Fush, found ourselves almost completely abandoning Pedro for the windmill, which, of course, had to operate outside.

Although prison fare was supposed to be below the level of our own, a level mighty hard to maintain and still keep body and soul incorporated, Fush and I shared and shared alike with Pedro. We saw to it that he got his twenty-five cents worth (that is, as near to it as a Patterson could get). Whereas Pedro's menu was supposed to read cornbread and molasses, sowbelly and black coffee only, we smuggled him up such delicacies as flour gravy, and sugar molasses, and *frijoles* for other meals. But from an old *compadre* of Pedro's who was allowed to visit him a few minutes one time, we learned that Pedro was holding his *frijoles* over for breakfast. And we learned from this *amigo* that Pedro liked them fried, after they were cooked, of course.

The very next morning Pedro got his *frijoles* fried, and he was so grateful the tears on that wide-spreading *mustacio* sparkled like crystal dew. In season, meaning when our seven cows would give milk (and give it down), Pedro would get cream for his coffee. And, occasionally, even sugar.

In return for Pedro's gifts, his concerts, and his congeniality we attempted to return his watch (or what we could find of it). He took the parts, reassembled them, set the watch to ticking again and gave it right back.

"I no go *no* place, No?" he said with logic, "so no need *reloj*."

If Fush was grateful, I was doubly so, realizing that but for Pedro Fush would be out somewhere risking *our* neck at some daredevil diversion or another.

In Pedro's case the wheels of justice seemed to grind exceeding slow—slower even than usual. So slowly, in fact, that the patient Pedro had begun to pace the cell floor. Papa, although no great shakes at psychiatry or jurisprudence, examined Pedro and pronounced him sane—not only sane but innocent. Thus exonerated, Pedro was given his freedom, by the simple expedient of turning a cell-door key.

His parole and the parting were sad for all of us. As far as Fush and I were concerned he could have moved downstairs with us. He was so little he couldn't eat much. We had no guest room, as such, no spare room, but he could sleep with Fush and me. And he would have had to sleep between us; we'd have fought like cats and dogs for the honor of sleeping next to him. As yet we hadn't heard too much about the stratum of society to which the herder was relegated. Nor had we heard too much about the Anglo, regardless of moral standards, social status being superior to any member of any minority race, regardless of the latter's birthright or high moral principles. Too, we were too young to have contracted race prejudice, a disease picked up only after some years of contact with contaminated adults. We were still at the face-value stage where love and admiration could penetrate any color of skin.

CHAPTER XX

Until Mama read us a newspaper article on sabotage we were hardly aware that there was a war on (World War I). Food rationing? Cornbread Wednesdays? Meatless Tuesdays? Sugarless Sundays? Old stuff to us. It didn't take a war to tell a family living in its twenty-eighth home in eighteen years that grub ought to be rationed.

The story in the El Paso *Sunday Herald*, datelined Detroit and headlined "BEWARE OF SABOTEURS" didn't shake Fush in the least. Not knowing what was a saboteur and where was Detroit he dismissed it with a yawn. Neither did I know what and where. But a cannonball through the courthouse cupola couldn't have alerted nor alarmed me more. This account told of German saboteurs sneaking around at night and slipping ground glass or arsenic into people's groceries. Staples only, I noticed, bitterness now sharing some billing with the alarm. But no time for brooding. Time for action. At my earliest convenience I must take preventive measures. Earliest convenience wasn't long in coming, what with Fush out seeking a war of his own, Gwen still small, Blanche visiting the Garners or the Lanes, and Mama back in a novel. Coast clear I rushed to the kitchen and skimmed off the top of the flour, sugar, baking powder, soda, and salt, thus saving at least five lives!

Almost delicious was that night's supper, consisting of the usual staples, plus a vinegar pie Mama baked (which we didn't consider a "fancy," vinegar being one of the cheapest commodities we bought). Vinegar pie! All of a sudden the thought of it triggered some terrifying moments that stretched into hours. My Lord, I had forgotten to pour off the top of the vinegar!

This staple-skimming and vinegar-pouring, however, was of few days duration and full of trouble. Fush, reading me like Mama read a book, caught me in the act. His ridicule proved sharper than ground glass in the stomach, more dreaded than a bayonet in the back. Made my act seem downright cowardly. Cowardly or no, I would probably have kept it up but for two reasons: One, I discovered that Mama had done the same thing immediately after reading the article (mine was the second skimming), and, two, Fush halfway convinced me it was unnecessary.

"The way Mama explains it—how I understand it—is that these saboteur fellers go around in wooden shoes. And have you seen any wooden shoe tracks lately? Besides, how could a feller in wooden shoes sneak across these concrete floors without Mama hearin' 'em?"

This menace overcome and done with, another one even more fierce and fearsome raised its head—Pancho Villa himself. Mad at President Wilson for taking up for Carranza, Pancho was threatening to fight his way to Washington and take over. Only recently he had raided New Mexico (farther from Upland than Old Mexico was) and had killed people on the Texas side of the river. In the Glen Springs raid, they say, it was some of his bunch that carried off our own Dr. Powers, who outmaneuvered them and got away.

As a result of Pancho's threat our part of the country was on the alert, Rankin and Upland included. Literate enough to read a geography map, I was horrified to discover that Upland lay exactly on a direct line between Chihuahua (Villa's hangout) and Washington D.C. (Wilson's). A ray of sunshine lit up, but only fleetingly, the dark, ominous cloud that encompassed me round about.

Maybe old Pancho would swing by Rankin to even the score with Dr. Powers. Not likely. The guard that old Doc had overpowered would be sent on that mission of vengeance. Old Villa would hold straight to his course. Result: wakeful nights alternating with nightmares. Awake or asleep I kept picturing Pancho and bloody *compadres* swooping down upon us one dark night, daggering us in our beds and making off with our hard-earned herd. How was he to know that old Whitey was too lazy to travel out of a walk, the mares couldn't pull the *sombrero* off your *cabeza* and the seven *vacas* wouldn't give a gallon of blue john *leche* a day? This would leave old Polecat the only critter of any value at all. But high-with-ered, anvil-headed, box-ankled and gimlet-rumped, he was too ugly for Pancho to parade to Washington on. The language barrier was all that kept me from wiring him, with some paraphrasing, the Old Testament quote attributed to Gideon: "Behold, Lord, our family is poor in *Upland*, and I am the least in my father's house." The fact that Gideon went on to face and overcome ten-thousand-to-one odds was of little comfort to me of little faith.

Mental pictures sharpened, anxieties deepened, when more intelligence reached us to the effect that Mexicanos (not the Pedro type, but the *Ladino* variety like the one who had preceded Pedro as our upstairs guest) were flocking into Rankin by the boxcar load. As a result Rankin had cleaned its guns, put on an extra night watchman and Mr. Garner had sent Papa a pearl-handled .45 pistol, a couple of .30-.30 rifles and plenty of ammunition. Though I was God-thankful for the weapons, I was put out at Mr. Garner about the *pearl-handled* pistol. Why not just a plain one? Why, a bright bauble like this would attract the likes of old Pancho as sugar molasses draws flies. Just as my active imagination didn't overlook a single potential protective measure, neither did it evade a single eventuality.

In Papa's, Sog's, and Alvin Reed's hands, then, rested the defense of Upland, capital of Upton County. Though I thought the world and all of Sog I was glad a horse fall had sprained his shoulder so he could be with us in this time of crisis, and I was doubly thankful to realize that it wasn't his shooting shoulder that was sprained.

Papa, Sog, and Alvin—three as brave defenders as an embattled county capital could have. And Fush could swap lead with them in a pinch. Here the thought suddenly occurred to me what a God's blessing godsend old Alvin was. Why, he'd fought "Meskins" all his life, even killed one or two, we'd heard said . . . . Oh, Lord, all the more reason for them to come to Upland! To finish Alvin off! But in the dark how could they tell Alvin from *me?* Which imaginings put me right back where I started, in a highly distraught state.

Daily, rumors grew more gruesome, making the menace much larger, with my imagination growing apace. Each night I went to bed wondering if Villa hadn't just killed off all of Rankin and was at that moment watering his jaded Spanish ponies in the B-Diamond tank, and dipping up water—mixed with blood—for himself in his deep-brimmed sombrero.

Then, one pitch-dark night it happened. Fush and I were brought upright in our bed by the sound of rapid gunfire and wild, *bandido*-sounding yells.

"Ay-yay yay yay. Yiyiyiyiyiy, eeeeeeeeeee ahhhhhhhhhh."

"Boom! Barooommmmm! Bang! Kapoom!" came reports from all kinds and calibers of guns.

Pancho and party. Not a doubt in the world. As security against Villa's gaining entrance Fush and I kept a chair propped against the door and pushed up snug underneath the door knob. This night we were especially pre-cautious since all the women were visiting Grandma Pollard, and the big men of the family were sleeping over in the courthouse. (Small comfort to me now to recall that Rufe Windham, another fearless recruit was an overnight guest of Papa's. What chance against this army?)

I lay there wondering how quick it would be; how Pancho's

men would go about the job; how sorry Papa would be for leaving me and Fush (seven and nine respectively) here by ourselves; how sorrowful and how ashamed of his race Pedro would be when he heard about it; how I would like to go out as brave as I knew Fush would. In fact, I mustered voice enough to voice these thoughts in part:

"Goodniss it, at Papa. Serve him right to find us dead in . . ."

Here my sorrowful surmise was chopped off short by the sudden rattling of the door under the impact of a heavy foot, accompanied by a few rapid, guttural words in an unknown tongue—Spanish, of course. Fush and I responded simultaneously but differently to that first shrill blast of Gabriel's trump. Fush jumped out of bed and grabbed something (it swished like a broom) with which to sell his life as dearly as possible. I burrowed back under the cover as far as I could, God-thankful that it was a feather mattress in which it was possible—though not probable—I could be overlooked.

"Don't let 'em in! Don't let 'em in!" It was more of a prayer to God than a command to Fush.

"'Bout as well git it over with," Fush said, his voice sounding, I imagine, like a condemned man ordering his last meal. Presently the door burst open under the Chihuahua-spurred boot—no doubt of it—of old Pancho himself. I closed my eyes waiting for the *navajazos*, or *balazos*, to do their messy work. There was a brief commotion. There went poor little brave Fush. Seems like he could have at least put up a better fight for me.

"Sog!" said a shrill voice. No, Fush is still in there fighting but calling for help.

"Jesus save . . ." I had no more than gotten my salutation through until the quilts were snatched from over my head. There, lantern in hand, stood not Pancho Villa but Sog.

"What's a matter, Paul? You look boogered, sort of." The understatement of the ages, by one prone to understatement. In this brief period of time every emotion known to psychiatry had stampeded through me, relief now predominating.

"But—but—but old Villa?"

"Whataye mean, old Villa? Can't a body celebrate New Year's around here, without people thinkin' they's a war on?"

CHAPTER XXI

From 1914 through 1917 God's weatherman sloshed the world's quota of rainfall down on the poor doughboys over in Europe's battlefields, where it wasn't needed, thus leaving the Southwest in the clutches of the worst drouth in Upland's recorded history. The JM, the Y, and John Garner's Greasewood brand lost thousands of cattle, with smaller ranches hit proportionately as hard.

One old cowman, with nothing left but a sense of humor put it this way: "Cattle dyin' so fast the buzzards are three weeks behind on eye balls and . . ." We interrupt just prior to the vulgarity but the expression is complete enough to give one a graphic picture of conditions. The cattle that survived the first year, he said, were a cinch to pull through. Immune now to every ailment except bone felon and skin mange.

It was during these times that Fush and I realized for a few fleeting days our ambition. We "got on" with a Mr. Cason who was moving a little drought-stricken herd to old Ma Reed's, some twenty miles west. Cowboys at last—even if we were bringing up the drags. But what a far cry from the big steer herd days of yore —cattle gaining weight as they went on belly-deep grass, and stampeding every night from pure animal spirits.

The herd, like a starving, beaten army plodded westward over powdery hills and across parched draws with only an occasional dusty wisp of buffalo grass to demand their attention. Bare dusty earth where green grass once waved, dew-sparkled and succulent at this time of morning. As for shrubs and brush only blackbrush and greasewood, survival of the fittest—catclaw, *corona de lagrima* (the Mexican's crown of thorns), chaparral, and of course mesquite. Mesquite, that range land immortal that not only survived but thrived on privation and hardship. In fact, it was in these times of crisis when it yielded its most bountiful crops. And its fruits were sweeter, safer for stock, and more nourishing.

"Looks like other poor herds have passed this way before us," Mr. Cason remarked, "and soonered us on the mesquite bean crop, otherwise known as the old Comanches' bread of life. So, we'll lift up our eyes unto the hills from whence cometh our deliverance." He had wound up with scripture to lift our spirits, I suppose. Whereas my spirits were already lifted, this tended to depress a bit. Lifted eyes caught sight of the buzzards, wheeling lazily, tirelessly overhead, hoping to spot, not signs of life but of death.

"Mr. Cason, why them old mean, nasty things?"

"God's creatures same as the medder lark, the peacock, and the eagle. And the quail. But for buzzards to clean up carrion the rest of us could die of a pestilence of some sort. Son, don't never sell any of God's creatures short." With still lifted eyes I counted the dust devils (whirlwinds) that built up and danced and twisted all over.

"Mr. Cason, what's that a sign of?"

"Sign there's apt to be a dry spell comin'."

Bound for Mr. Cason to come up with something cheerful. He was gentle, patient—a good man for little cowboys to work for, which latter word brought me back to the business at hand—punching up the drags. Slobbering baby calves had to be prodded from beneath every bush and with no hoodlum wagon along to haul them, many had to be abandoned to the coyotes. Their mothers, the mother instinct starved within them, reeled ahead with scarcely a backward glance, knowing that the next bush could well be their last resting place. Now and then an old cow would drop out and lie down and give up the ghost. Generally the younger cows would carry on if lifted to their feet—tailed up. To any other cowboy or cowman alive a deeply depressing scene indeed, but not to Fush and me. Though Fush would have preferred some "rippin', stavin', and stompedin'," I was perfectly content with this snail's pace. I could keep the drags moving and still keep count on the whirlwinds swirling across the seared plains.

The herd snailed on westward through the veil of dust and dancing heat waves. By now the midday sun's rays, deflected upward from the naked alkali had seared our faces and raised blisters on our lips. We had long since drained our canteens, and thirst was getting quite a grip upon us. But since this was a cowboy job there was nothing I could dare say or do about it.

"But it does look like . . ."

Oh, oh. There was Fush right over there. To appear to be taking it as well as he was, I better shut up.

Around midafternoon the herd topped a low rise, and there in a draw, wheeling lazily under a gentle breeze were two big Eclipse windmills. Goaded by the smell of water, the leaders broke into a shambling trot. The weaker drags quickened their pace as best they could. Soon the herd was milling around the tank. Ordinarily the tank would have been fenced off, but previous herds had trampled it down. Mr. Cason rode herd on them while we were watering our horses. But for an unwritten law of the range, I'd have tied my mount to the handiest bush and drunk my fill first. As soon as the code would permit, Fush and I scrambled up the tank dump where the lead pipe was spilling its cool stream. Leaning out over the mossy water we cupped the stream with a free hand and drank until our breath played out, rested and drank again. Shortly, up jingled Mr. Cason with one of his philosophical remarks:

"They say the German prefers his beer, the Mexican his tequila, the Italian his *vino*, the Irishman anything with a wallop, but give me windmill nectar any old time, a drink brewed by the angels.

With this off his chest he dropped to the lead pipe and drank until he barely had the strength to muscle himself back up. Then we rode out to the chuck wagon and partook of our sowbelly, beans, and King Komus molasses. A cowboy now, I couldn't let on, but I was bitterly disappointed, to say the least.

By late afternoon my spirits were in keeping with the scene—a scene and setting more grim, more depressing than that of the morning. To the sight of death now was added the smell of it from the carcasses of previous herds. What with a breeze in our faces, the stench was enough to bring up my sowbelly and beans. By now cows who had abandoned their calves had relented and were beginning to turn back and bawl. So was I, but softly. Fush and Mr. Cason must not know. Fush would laugh me to scorn and Mr. Cason would fire me. (Would that be so bad? Better disgrace than death, dishonor before dehydration.) Here I was destined, determined to be a cowboy and practically undone the first day out. I, who at seven years of age, had moved in a covered wagon ten, twelve times within the scope of my own memory in all kinds of weather eating all kinds of chuck (except fancy) sleeping in all kinds of camps, but might not last the day . . . .

"Why hadn't Papa and Sog told me . . . ?"

But blaming them didn't seem to give me relief. The dust was blinding my eyes, the alkali was searing my lungs, the sun was cooking my lips, the thirst was torturing my throat, and the saddle was killing my behind.

"Paul, we're makin' a killin' on this trip. Dollar apiece a day!"

"Killin' is right," I muttered gruffly and reined away so as to hide the tears.

After endless, hope-sapping hours we reached another windmill, watered out and threw the herd into a fence corner for the night with Mr. Cason and the cook to stand night guard. This would be a busy, all-night job keeping the hungry herd on the bed grounds.

CHAPTER XXII

A few days after our eventful trail drive and the subsequent race against stark starvation, another drought-stricken herd snailed through Upland. The boss of this outfit left us an old bone bag of a Mexican cow to care for until he passed back through. Now, it is the nature of the cow brute, like some people, to bite the hand that is feeding her, to knock down the Samaritan that lifts her up. The first time Fush and I started toward this critter with feed and water, she snuffed, lowered her wide, sharp horns and made for us. I dropped the bucket of water and skedaddled. After I had reeled off a fast fifty yards or so I heard a loud *throomppp!* Without breaking stride I looked back to see the old cow flat and kicking and Fush standing like a bony Tarzan of the apes with one foot on her side. Only difference was, it was the cow that was bellering. Fush, in self defense, had felled the old heifer with a rock. Until she passed on to the perpetual sweet grass country she had to have breakfast in bed.

Now we had, I figured, a murder on our hands, and the old panics began to well up in me. Horse-stealing, they said, called for hanging. Maybe cow-killing, I reasoned, would call for the same sentence. Cows ate grass like horses, didn't they? Reasoning thus, I worked myself up into a highly distraught state of mind and stayed that way. Fush, on the other hand, could dismiss frets and bothers from his mind as completely as Miz Ham dismissing school. His autopsy, he assured me, showed not a mark of violence on that old cow. All evidence and indications pointed to only one conclusion—death by stark starvation. Case dismissed.

The day after the old cow's demise we spied an approaching horseman. To me, he sat his saddle like a Texas Ranger. But Fush recognized him as the late cow's (late) owner. That he was the owner and not a Ranger was little consolation. If the owner comes, can the Ranger be far behind?

"She's dead," I hollered when the man was still two hundred yards away, hoping to steer him away from the scene of the crime. Too, I didn't want him close enough to read my dead-giveaway expression.

"Oh, Lord, wilst Thou but turn him aside?" I prayed, desperately, but he kept coming on. However, as if in partial answer to my prayer he reined in and flipped each of us a silver dollar.

"Knowed the old heifer was done fer when I left her here. Jist wanted her last days easier. You fellers done me a good job. Much oblige."

Without so much as a glance in the direction of the old cow's remains, he spurred away, leaving us two dollars richer and me feeling that I had just beaten the hangman by a neck!

CHAPTER XXIII

Upland during the big drought typified the old saying, "Out where the cows cut the wood and the wind hauls the water." With no rain to dissolve and wash away the cow chips, they cured into a splendid, slow-burning fuel, just the thing for heating wash water. As to the cooking of meals, however, they were a miserable substitute for mesquite wood, unless one preferred cow chip smoked sowbelly—not to mention a wall-to-wall-smoked kitchen. Since frankness of expression had not yet spread beyond cow camps and mule-skinners' conventions (and the writings thereof had come no closer to the parlor than outhouse walls), in company such fuel was referred to as "grassolene."

Hauling grassolene was our chore, and a distasteful one it was unless we had company. But when June Garner or Pat and Bill Collins and Lee Lane, or all of them together were visiting us it was a different colored horse. Then we'd hook old Whitey to the buckboard, drive down the JM draw and square off for a cow chip battle. By mutual agreement the bigger, more lethal ones called "gray flats" were ruled out—too inhumane. But the smaller ones, the "brown rounds" were used profusely as mortars, grenades, bazooka fire, and even bayonets at close range.

On September 1, 1917, a half mile north of the JM horse corrals the biggest, bitterest, bloodiest cow chip battle of the decade took place, opposing forces consisting of every child citizen and former citizen of Upland. I was the first casualty, the first to go down under the withering fire of the enemy (typical of me, I withered almost before the enemy fired). Opposing generals called a temporary truce in order to clear the battlefield of the disabled, namely me.

Suffering at the top of my lungs, I was led to the shade of a chaparral bush and administered to by Fush and Bill Collins. Summoning as much coherence as I could muster I denounced the enemy for violating civilized rules of warfare as laid down by the Geneva convention. I maintained, and stoutly, that I had been hit up side the head by a much heavier "cowliber" missile than regulations allowed. Fush, knowing the caliber of my fortitude, was skeptical; he figured it was merely shell shock, a cracking of the nerves. Bill Collins wasn't so sure.

"Fush, I do believe he's out'n his head—*on*conscious," he said uneasily.

"Naw, I don't believe so," Fush said, turning to me, "but I'll make for shore, Paul, whichaway's Upland?"

"Bawwwwwwww. Awwwwwwww."

"Come on, Paul, what color is old Whitey?"

"Booooooooo. Ohhhhhhhhhh. Awwwwww."

Fush turned away disgusted but relieved. "Paul's all right. Long as he can bawl like that I know he's healthy and in his right mind."

He clouted General Collins with a solid chunk of fertilizer, and the battle was rejoined—though I didn't rejoin it. From my vantage point beneath and behind a big mesquite I commanded a splendid view of the battle, that is, until darkness rendered visibility zero.

Only one other cow chip hauling ever engendered more excitement than the above, and it involved only three of us—Fush, myself, and Lee Lane. There weren't enough recruits to start a cow chip battle (one reason I consented to go along), but I should have known Fush would start *something*. Which he did. Something that was really something—a prairie fire.

A perfectly innocent-appearing something at first, as all of Fush's enterprises started—a mere woodrat's nest fire. It was really hilarious to see the poor old wood rats dart out in all directions as from a burning barn, or a sinking ship. How funny to see them scatter, but not after the fire began to scatter too.

"Prairie fireeeeeeeee," Lee hollered, a pronouncement about as necessary as the age-old question "are you asleep?" For by this time birds, rabbits, ground squirrels, and other small animals were leaving like rats from a burning barn. The gravity of the situation was evidenced by old Whitey's showing signs of stompeding, and by Lee's and Fush's lighting into the spreading flame, the former with his brand new corduroy coat and the latter with a big brown, fuzzy fedora that was his pride and joy. Only after superhuman efforts on their part (and considerable running and bawling on mine) plus the fact that a fairly wide arroyo intervened, did *we* bring the blaze under control.

A brief, breathless assessment revealed considerable damage—a couple acres of the town section burned off, a brand new corduroy coat riddled with holes, and a fine, once-fuzzy fedora now, slick, sooty, and floppy as could be.

"Could be worse," said the ever-optimistic Lee, scarcely able to restrain outright laughter at the ridiculous figure Fush now cut in his once-fine, once-fuzzy fedora.

"And will be," added the realistic Fush, "when we get home." It was.

CHAPTER XXIV

To all intents and purposes Upland was dead, although not yet so legally and officially. Had it been buried in its own graveyard along with Old Man Olmstead, Mrs. Judge Ainsworth, and the Blanton baby, the date on its headstone would have read 1910–1916. Good Lord! Here it was late 1918! Which meant that we were nearly three years with the dead and couldn't tell it; three years with a corpse and couldn't smell it. But those closest to a situation are the last to find out or to admit it or accept it when they do.

We should have begun to suspect something after months had passed without our jail having accommodated a single upstairs boarder. But we just figured it was like Sog said, "Nothin' like Patterson grub to set a man back on the straight and narrow. Or to cure him of the calaboose, at least." Nor did it occur to us that something was amiss when all county offices except the treasurer's (Papa's) had been operating out of the Rankin schoolhouse for a year or more. It was only after the county commissioners, Upland's most active and devoted servants, ceased to hold forth here anymore, that we realized something was amiss:

I, the least perceptive of all, was, ironically, the first to notice. Perhaps it was because the commissioners' courtroom (where Sog stumbled onto that jug) was my favorite haunt, hangout, or hide-

out, whichever the case might warrant. It just wasn't its old throb-
bing, dynamic self. How could I tell? By the usual means—sight,
sound, and smell, the latter sense of which I always placed more
reliance upon. Vivid flashbacks into my fifteen, twenty, or twenty-
five previous homes were always associated more with smells than
with the other two combined.

As regards the courtroom, its view from the southwest window
is, was, and ever shall be the same—an ever-gripping panorama of
sweeping, greenish-brown hills with the dim blue bulk of King
Mountain as a back drop. And the high, cool, green walls were the
same, except for clusters of initials, predominantly WFPs and PIPs
with an occasional LRL, JWG, BC, PC scratched through the
green and deep into the white of the plaster.

And the solid oak chairs, with positively unbreakable, unremov-
able, unscratchable arms, were the same and would ever remain so.
Likewise the long, light oak table, except for more WFPs and PIPs
and numerous examples of very crude and primitive art (done in
penknife or nail) depicting a very primitive type of cowboy at
work and at play.

Except for the scrape of five chairs on concrete, the chatter and
the banter of judge and commissioners, with or without court in
session, the sounds were about the same—the lonesome wind ever
sawing and sighing at the sharp edges of courthouse objects, and
the ever lonesome cry of the coo-coo bird during summer afternoon sessions (as opposed to the brisk, friendly crackling of the
fireplace in winter). Sounds now prevalent, though missing during
sessions, would be the long-drawn-out zooooommmmmmmPHT!
from cupola platform down to the bottom of the roof ledge. That
would be Fush taking the roof slide. Standing up.

So much for sight and sound. It was by the commissioners' courtroom smell that I could tell Upland was dead. It wasn't the stench
of death, nauseating and repulsive; in fact, it was the same pleasant,
cool concrete smell as always. But missing were the overtones that
bespoke of activity, vitality—the aroma of living, so to speak. Gone

was the entrancing aroma of just-lit cigars, of smoke from a fresh-poured, home-rolled Bull Durham, of an about-to-be-bit-off-of plug of Tinsley, Thick or Thin, of new Stetsons ringing the rack, of right-off-the-counter ducking pants, and of shop-made boots yet to lose their new leather, fresh-polish fragrance.

The joy of being a romanticist and idealist is that you are forever spared the harsh, the brutal realities of the past and the future (though sometimes the present will pester you). Consequently, only the commissioners' court aromas ever assail the nostrils of memory, uninvoked. As for the unpleasant lower stages of aroma such as smell, odor, and stink, they won't return unless summoned. Consequently, again, it never occurred to me that I had likewise been subjected to cigars, Bull Durham cigarettes, Thick and Thin Tinsley, Stetsons, ducking pants, and boots in their lower stages.

For example, take this fine Havana cigar, the closer the ash end moves to the chewed end the aroma becomes less and less like an aroma and more and more like a smell. And when this fine Havana becomes too wet to stay lit it deteriorates into an odor. Finally, when it can no longer serve even as a chaw it is tossed into the spittoon. Then and there is where it begins to stink. The same can be said of Bull Durham and Tinsley. Just as the same can be said of Stetsons, ducking pants, and shop-made boots, especially the latter. Take the briefest of strolls through a branding pen, for example. Now your new boot aroma has given way to smell, with only faint overtones of aroma remaining. Ride, walk, stand, or sleep a day or so in these boots, remove them and your smell will evince undertones of odor, with no overtones of aroma left. Persist in this and first thing you know you have a pair of once-aromatic boots that stink.

Upland was dead but didn't stink. Eventually, however, Papa began to smell a mouse, which fact was to have far reaching effects on Patterson peace and prosperity for all time to come. As soon as Papa realized that the upstairs boarder business was "blowed up" and that courthouse business was no more, he got authorization from the commissioners' court to write himself out his final checks for services rendered as jailer and sheriff's office deputy. But he would still have that $300 rolling in every year of the world as county treasurer.

Papa's next move was to move—move number *twenty-nine*. And, strange as it may sound, he dreaded it; he dreaded it more than any and all the other moves he'd ever made. This was because of how Mama was going to take it—if she took it.

For eighteen long hard years, and twenty-eight long hard moves Mama had dreamed of running water, of kitchen sinks (zincs, she called them), of lavatories, and most especially of a room where nothing had to be carried into or carried out of. She couldn't conceive of a greater blessing than a bathtub that filled itself up unless it was a pot that emptied itself out. How thankful-proud she was of this "closet," as she called it, scolding us in almost stern tones for our various and varied titles for it: "indoor outhouse," "squat pot," "inside flush." Papa's name "privvy" was even frowned upon. (Never was the four-letter word read aloud on this type of accommodation's walls, much less utilized as a title.)

CHAPTER XXV

Small comfort to Mama that number twenty-nine was to be only one hundred yards north across the courthouse square to the abandoned telephone office. Speculation was rife as to whether Mama would make another move. "She's not gonna part with that indoor outhouse for love nor money." said Sog. He was half right. Only after the old telephone office was revived as an exchange for Midland, Rankin, and surrounding ranches, and Mama was put on as an operator did she consent to move. Who wouldn't—at a beyond-one's-wildest-dreams salary of $10 per month?

What with her superior education—superior for those times—she had finally hit upon something she could do and enjoy. Do, yes, but not always enjoy, as it turned out. Telephones were susceptible to lightning, another of God's natural elements that Mama had an unnatural horror of. Yes, she was afraid, even after Sog had showed her the three-pronged "lightning arrester" fastened high upon the wall phone's forehead.

Being the daughter of a Methodist circuit riding preacher Mama wasn't one to even banter the Lord's name about much less take His name in vain, so when Sog asked, "Mama, who made lightnin', God or the devil?" he was taking the wrong tack.

"Go—the Lord, of course. But don't you ever, . . ." Mama

shouted, glancing fearfully in His direction as if expecting a bolt directly from the blue.

"Well, if Go—if He made lightnin' instead of the old d—bad man, why be afraid . . . ?"

"Don't ever . . . , I said," Mama shouted, now verging on the jaw-boxing stage.

Sog's next approach was to get the catalog and have Mama read aloud the peerless performing qualities of their *New Two-Path Carbon Lightning Arrester*, "the most perfect protection from lightning as well as sneak currents, that has ever been devised by man. This arrester is made up of three heavy brass punchings . . . ."

Here Mama laid the book aside with an aside of her own: "Brass, gold, silver, whatever, I still don't trust the thing. And, John, honey, don't water the ground wire—let the thing pop and snap—long's it's hearable at all—I knew a man in Andrews County one time . . ."

To make a point Mama invariably and inevitably wound up with an example—or rather three examples in one, none of which we could bear to stay and hear out with their limitless ramifications, involvements, intertwinings, and entanglements. As Sog said, "Nobody in Mama's dust when it comes to un-tellin' a story, or un-explainin' a situation." What he meant was that Mama was too prone to start in the middle and tell three ways.

Meantime, back at the telephone exchange, Mama was finding a situation—aside from the lightning—with which she hardly knew how to cope. This was the party liners, they yielded to *nobody* when it came to talking or to yielding line. Well there was somebody they would yield line to—Ike Stovall down at the JM. Ike had the vocabulary of a modern best seller novelist and wouldn't hesitate to use it—even in a day and time when I got slapped away from the table for saying "bob-tail bull," and when the word "leg" as applied to the female limb was downright obscene, not to say profane.

But Ike actually proved the worst of two evils, so what exactly was she to do when, say, Mr. Bishop wanted the line open so he could close a big JM cattle deal (four, five, six thousand yearlings) with Bob Hill, of Midland? Nothing, she figured, except gather her neatly filled out call slips, catch the mail car to Midland and turn them in—along with her resignation. But just as lightning was about to strike, figuratively, a silver-lined, lightning-free cloud appeared. Some cowman on the line complimented Mama: "Lady, please don't consider me forward, but could I pay you a compliment?"

"Why, Yes!"

"You've got the finest speakin' voice ever I heard over a telephone line."

"Why . . ."

"On top of that, I can tell you are a woman of refinement."

"Why, er. Compliment received, duly considered, and deeply appreciated . . ."

"You know, Ma'am—I don't want to call you Central—you're the first operator yet to say 'just a minute' right and proper. With the others it's 'jist a minit' or 'hold yer horses,' or some such."

Not since Bob Dickey had complimented Mama's biscuits back in '14 had Mama heard a compliment. Compliments were few and far between at our house—sounded too much like bragging to Papa. Just as Mama's biscuits, as well as the other staples and the occasional vinegar pie, had improved 50 per cent, so did Upland telephone service from that day forward. Party liners, barbwire telephone lines, poorly grounded phones, faulty lightning arresters, and lightning itself notwithstanding, messages went through without delay—not even "just a minute." As a specific example Sog stayed on the line thirty minutes whistling *Steamboat Bill* to keep it open for Rufe Bishop, JM boss, on one end. And, who knows, perhaps the *complimenter* on the other.

Although we didn't know it at the time, there was an incentive just as great, or greater even than the complimenter that kept Mama hanging in there through lightning, long hours, and party liners. Mama was hoarding for the most momentous move of her life—that move toward total independence. Or as Sog later put it, "pulling that picket pin—permanent." Ironically, or prophetically, her chance came three days before Independence Day of 1919. With $40 of her very own and with Papa off building fence, Blanche visiting in Rankin, Sog and Fush on the way to New Mexico with a John R. Johnston trail herd there was nobody to block Mama's path to freedom except little Gwen and myself. Even so, she was taking no chances on muffing her one great opportunity of a lifetime—freedom. She got us out of Upland under guise of "going to your Grandma Pollards for a little visit."

"You would like that wouldn't you?"

I certainly would. Anywhere on earth would beat Upland right now, with Fush gone. How very very dead Upland was. But then I supposed any town without Fush would be dead.

It wasn't until we missed the Andrews-bound mail car out of Midland and were on the east-bound Texas & Pacific passenger train that she told us: "We are parting from your Papa."

I had already suspected as much but was too completely, absolutely awestruck by the deliciously frightening experience of a train ride. However, the gravity of the situation was brought home by the wording of the message.

"I say, children, we're parting from your Papa."

"You are. Me and Gwen are not. Never. We want to go home. Right now." Already the awesomely delicious sights, sounds, smells, and sensations of the train were gone—drowned out, dimmed by the wash of tears, muffled by an all encompassing sorrow. Gwen didn't have anything to say but her tears were most eloquent, so eloquent, in fact, that Mama joined us, making it a trio. Mama, mindful of our feelings, didn't silence us. Or press her point. But it was obvious her mind was made up—total independence or nothing. Her ticket was definitely one way.

My very first train ride, my very first sight of big towns, my very first sight of rivers, my very first opportunity to purchase any of the exotic wares of the news butch should have and could have left me in a state of pure exultation. But I was aware only of a great emptiness, a pressing, depressing sorrow that seemed to have no end, no solution this side of the grave. Papa and the others wouldn't know where we had gone. We would never see them and Upland again. And if we did see them it would mean that we wouldn't see Mama any more. Why couldn't Papa and Mama have loved each other like they both loved us?

Big towns, little towns, big rivers, little rivers, creeks—all a swimming blur, such was my sorrow. The names, however (Stanton, Big Spring, Colorado City, Loraine, Roscoe, Sweetwater, Hamlin, Benjamin, Medicine Mound), took on distinction, if not significance, strictly from the most peculiar way they were called out. Something like "Taylor, whyn't ye getche a new saiddleeee?" (*Must* tell Fush this just as soon as I see him. If I ever do.) Had the towns been called out in the normal, ordinary manner, only one would have held any significance to me—Big Spring. That was where Aunt Zo lived. I so wished I had some way of getting word to her to get word to Papa. But what good would that do? I don't know myself where we are going to. Mama won't tell us.

We wound up in Altus, Oklahoma, a sandy, gloomy, steamy place with no windmills, no rolling plains, no broncs tied here and there, no men with spurs on, no nothing, it seemed to me, except a bunch of town dudes in caps and a few old clodhoppers in overalls and farm wagons. On top of that the Altus kids turned out mean to fight.

"Wisht I had Fush here to show these clodhoppers a thing or two," I lamented, tearfully. Shortly, I was to have a small measure of revenge. The young telegraph operator, whose boardinghouse room was just across the hall from ours, rushed in with the wire saying that Jack Dempsey had just knocked out Jess Willard, an Oklahoman. Not that I knew who Jack Dempsey was or what they were fighting about, or cared. The fact that the Oklahoma fellow got whipped was enough for me.

Dreary day upon dreary day—not to mention the weltering, sweltering July nights—piled one upon the other. Even a steady diet of straight-out "fancies"—cookies, crackerjacks, jams, peanut butter, crackers, candy (which we were allowed to eat in bed, if we so chose) weren't enough to appease me, to blunt the sharp edge of my grief. The same could be said of Gwen, little as she was. Oh, for a reunion with Papa and the others, oilcloth table of simple staples notwithstanding.

To add insult to injury, to rub salt in the wounds, so to speak, I overheard Mama tell a prospective employer, a big farmer in overalls, she would keep house for three dollars a week and I, "stout for my size," could work for my board. Me, a cowboy, clodhopping on a farm? That did it. I exerted so much pressure on Mama she finally consented for me to write Papa (under provision that I tell him nothing personal).

The writing of this letter to Papa was for Gwen and me a silver lining in our dark clouds, a harbor in our perpetual storm, so to speak. But only a temporary one. More dreary days and sweating, sweltering nights without one word from Papa, which fact prompted from me my favorite self-pitying expression: "Doggone Papa. It'd serve him right if me and Gwen never did get home." Not that I wanted Papa to get "served right." The term was used in pure desperation, for Mama had finally landed a housekeeping job on this farm where I was to work for my board. The farmer was due to pick us up in the buggy day after tomorrow.

Here, even my agile imagination which had always stood me in good stead, couldn't extract me from this "slough of despond," couldn't project me across the corn patches and cotton pickers to New Mexico with Sog and Fush and the John R. trail herd—drawing six bits a day as horse jingler in Fush's place so he could move up to a dollar-a-day cowboy job alongside of Sog.

Nothing left to do now but wait and hope and pray and kick

the wall and cry, the latter of which I engaged in more than the former, and with a right ill will. In fact, wall-kicking and crying became my only pastime—it couldn't be called a diversion, especially by the young night shift telegraph operator across the hall, who was trying to get some sleep. Late one unbearably hot afternoon he bribed me to go out after a sack of Bull Durham plus any "fancy" my heart might fancy with the change left over. The bribe wouldn't have worked except that Mama's more than generous allowance had come to a sudden, abrupt unexplained stop nearly a week ago. Not like Mama at all.

On my way downstairs I met the landlady Mrs. Kincaid on her way up and seemingly in a high state of excitement. Dismissing it as a woman's natural state, I paid it no mind until she said to me, "Paul, honey, don't you go down there until I see your mother."

I wasn't one to disobey an order from anybody, but Mrs. Kincaid was probably just trying to protect my innocence from what I might see downstairs. In my state of mind what should I care if I had to step across dead bodies clear across the lobby floor. Mrs. Kincaid made only a half-hearted reach for me and hurried on upstairs. Oblivious to my surroundings I continued down the stairs. Suddenly, my downcast eyes picked up a rare sight—a pair of cowboy boots. Cowboy boots in the cotton country? Impossible! Nope, there they were, and spur marks on the heel pieces.

Gripped by a surge of curiosity, the first in many a week, my eye followed the boots to their tops, up the pants leg and to the face above them. *It was Papa!* So that was why the landlady was so excited. Evidently Mama had pictured Papa as a violent man and she was forewarning her. Either that or to give Mama a chance to hide us. God forbid! I was too elated, too overwhelmed to wonder how, what, where, or when. There he was with that same old eye-squinting smile, a smile made wider by a thick cud of Tinsley. Before I had even halfway said hello, little Gwen had bounced downstairs and pried me loose.

The violence that Mrs. Kincaid, and others, seemed to anticipate, didn't take place. The final meeting was cordial and the settlement agreeable. It was simply a matter of letting us choose, which, in a way, is the most brutal, the most heart-rending agreement of all.

"Pots, Paul's done said he wants to go home with me. Do you want to, too?"

"Yes, Papa. Oh, yes," Gwen said, with a neck lock on Papa a wrestler couldn't have broken.

"When you go home with me I'll buy you a doll. And your Mama can come too if she wants to."

"Yeah, Mama, why not?"

"Oh, Mama, please do!"

A gap of hushed, expectant silence as every eye turned in her direction, eagerly anticipating her reply, which wasn't long in coming though it seemed a couple of eternities. She shook her head "no." "Total independence" after those long, long years of moving misery stood beckoning like the siren's song.

In spite of how Gwen and I thought about Mama recently for running away with us, the separation, now a reality, was wringing the very heart out of us. And the sadness seemed contagious, for when the final words were said, there wasn't a dry eye in the crowd from the telegraph operator on down.

En route home we ate in a railroad cafe at Sweetwater, saw our first moving picture show (cowboys, Indians, and all) between a change of trains, but kept badgering Papa until he had to take us back to the depot, afraid we'd miss our train for home. Just as Mama had done, Papa let us buy all sorts of baubles and bonbons from the news butch. We did many unheard of things, saw many unheard of sights. But we were still not impressed, even when Papa ran his head out the window and his hat blew off up around Medicine Mound, too torn up over the separation and too anxious to get back to the other kids and the old way of life.

Once back in Upland I was beginning to be my old self again. Sog and Fush, bushy of hair and blistered of lip, had just ridden in off the trail. I immediately filled Fush with elaborated accounts of train travel, big cities, big rivers, picture shows, and how I had manhandled the dudes and clodhoppers up in Oklahoma. Fush could have reciprocated with stirring accounts of horse jingling up the trail but as usual allowed me the floor. Instinctively, he must have done the right thing, for, once all these greatly exaggerated experiences were off my chest I found that I didn't want to think of them, or speak of them ever again. They were a part of the past I never wanted to recall, except in emergencies.

To a great extent Blanche had assumed the duties of a mama for the last several years. Now she had taken over the responsibilities, even unto the whaling of me and Fush when the occasion, or our orneriness, demanded. For a sixteen-year old she did a marvelous job of it, in spite of the opposition we offered. Occasionally, however, we showed up at school with a considerable portion of Upton County clinging to neck and ears. But a young girl can't be expected to always gather two outlaws going in two directions at once. Blanche, with youth, enthusiasm, and good health in her favor, turned out to be a better cook and housekeeper than Mama. But in so doing she could use up more stovewood and more water (and more cow chips for washing) in a day than two kids "stout for their sizes" could cut, haul, and tote in a week.

CHAPTER XXVI

"Fush, you and Paul come run into Rankin with us," Bill Collins invited, "we're goin' to the Christmas Tree."

"What's a Christmas Tree?" Fush asked, "Somethin' that don't never shed its leaves?"

"Aw, crazy, come on. Old Santy'll be there."

"Who's she?" Fush asked again, knowing better in both cases but never having particularly benefited from either.

"Gawddern it, Fush, quit actin' silly and come on," Bill said, enough of Old Ma in him to express himself in terms as strong as the situation might demand.

"We don't have the money," Fush said, admitting things to Bill Collins that he wouldn't have admitted to anyone else.

Bill reached in his pocket and flipped each of us a half dollar. "Now gawddern it, you can't say that. Let's git goin'."

"I was jokin', Bill. Much oblige, but it ain't that," Fush lied, forcing the half back on Bill, which gesture forced me to do likewise.

"Dammit to hell, then, Fush, what is it?" Bill yelled, tearing another leaf from his grandma's vocabulary.

"Aw..."

"We're in a brand, spankin' new Four automobile," Bill laid

down his trump card, "and Mama and Pat and Sudie are out there with the engine a-runnin'."

"Go—sh dern it, then, Bill. Whyn't ye say so in the first place?" Fush squalled, almost tearing another leaf from Old Ma's vocabulary.

"Blanche, can we?"

"Yes. But put on your coats. And don't act a fool down there."

"Hello, Fush, Paul."

"How'd do, Miz Collins," and as an afterthought, or rather a forethought, "this shore is a crackerjack automobile."

Mrs. Collins, or Callie, was looked upon by some as too "mannish" and weather-beaten because she broke her own broncs. But if this were their reason, it enhanced her with me more than ever. Callie could help fill that fearsome void left by the departure of Sis and Mabel.

The lavish, glittering packages on and under the tree, the gaiety and laughter plus Santa Claus in the flesh, instilled in Fush and me a Christmas spirit exceeded by none. But not for long. At the halfway mark we sat surrounded by happy kids who were in turn surrounded by stacks of glittering presents. So far neither of us had received an apple, let alone the usual blue elephant piggy bank. Now old Santa had only three presents to go. About this time Fush got up and scuttled for the door. But I stayed on, faintly hopeful of receiving one of these last gifts. Two more to go. I tried desperately to catch old Santa's eye. No business. He handed the next-to-last one to a kid with a whole church full of presents, keeping the last one for himself. Hard put to keep from bawling, I bolted out to join Fush.

"It ain't that we wanted stuff to play with," Fush lamented, "It's just, just that I hate for people to know we're so gaw—doggone pore." His eyes were the nearest thing to crying since the Mustang Gray episode.

"Me too," I gritted, feeling a bitterness toward Old Santa that had heretofore been reserved for turtle-top straws.

The Collinses, Lee Lane, June Garner, and another kid or two came dashing out to the car.

"Fush," Bill said, "Ol' Sandy misread this'n. It turned out to be yores."

"And here's one for Paul, too." June Garner was saying, "Old Santy's eyes musta been half out!"

"Either that or he didn't give a dern," Lee Lane put in. "He got mixed up and give me one of Paul's too."

They crowded half a dozen packages at us, all of which Fush emphatically, but diplomatically, refused.

"Doggone it, Fush," I whispered, as bitter at him as I was at Santa, "why didn't you take them packages? They give 'em to us."

"Because they were not ours. And besides, Papa would make us send 'em back anyhow, when he got home." Fush said. Then as an afterthought, "Biggest dern liars in the world—them kids. Bless their hearts."

When Callie Collins got the auto under way she reached over and kissed me and Fush both. Bronc rider or not, she was all woman that night, for when she leaned down to take hold of us her face was wet.

"Papa can't help it about your Christmas," Blanche said, "so hush." Then as an afterthought. "Lord knows he works hard enough."

"If he works so hard, why can't we have lots for Christmas like other kids?" I whined.

"Well, Papa, bless his heart, is not very good in a deal, or a con-tract. Too honest. Tries always to give a day-and-a-half's work for a half-a-day's pay."

"That ain't my fault."

"Neither is it Papa's."

"Who's fault is it then, Mama's?" I snapped.

"Well, yes, and no. Yes, because, poor Mama, she couldn't man-age a lick in the road. Never could, they say, especially after I was born. Why, I've seen her take and burn up perfectly good clothes, throw 'em right down on the cow chips, because she didn't feel like washin' 'em."

"I never saw Mama burn up no clothes," I said, rising to her defense. It was nearly the truth. I'd never see her burn up anything except one pair of my drawers (winter, of course); the ones I had on the night I thought Pancho Villa had me. But nobody, even God Himself, would expect me to admit that. Would they?

Missing Mama more than I realized I found myself taking up for her.

"We'd be well off, Mama says, if Papa knew how to trade. One time he traded a four-section claim—four good sections of land—for a five-room house in Midland, then, some way, just burnt the house down. Burnt it down. Stuff like that."

"Who are you to blame people for burnin' houses down?"

"I, we didn't do it on purpose."

"Neither did Papa. Nor that other time when we burnt out close to Sterling City."

"You mean we been burnt out three times?"

"Three times. And that's partly our trouble now. That's what's to blame, really. Nobody's fault. You know, it seems hard to believe but some say, the Ouija Board does, that people get about what they deserve." When that kid in Rankin, known to be one of the meanest, with a half-churchhouse full of gifts . . . My silence to Blanche's statement wasn't voluntary, it was that I was just shocked, outraged into speechlessness. Whether we deserved it or not Santa did come two weeks later bringing the usual blue piggy bank for each and a few apples and nuts. It wasn't much, of course, but worth it to have Papa home.

CHAPTER XXVII

To a kid like Fush addicted to year-round action, there were only three respectable seasons—summer, spring, and fall, named in order of preference. Being as how it was generally a period of inertia, or indoor activity at most, winter was strictly for the birds, or rather the bears, snakes, and other hibernating creatures, not fit for man or decent beast. Consequently, Fush and Old Man Winter were mortal enemies, eternally at each others' throats (except that time, briefly, on January 16, 1914, when they collaborated, albeit unintentionally, in burning down the Taylor place). However, Fush and the winter of 1918–19 started out on excellent terms, with the latter having furnished us just the right amount of snow to make quail and rabbit hunting a cinch; enabling us and Lee Lane to chase down a mess of blues without expending a single shell. What's more, it afforded us a very humane type of snowball, a ball that wouldn't harden into a rocklike chunk of ice on impact and then immediately trickle down you in icy streams, a missile that was much more to my liking than cow chips, or even semi-rotten gourds.

"Yes sir, the first ol' winter out of ten to show a body any consideration," Fush had remarked, mellowing to winters in general and this one in particular, more tolerant than ever before of its tempests and its temperatures. Little did he dream that this was winter's way of throwing him off guard, softening him for the mortal struggle that lay ahead, and then aiming for the jugular, which it did violently and soon.

Mantled in a blinding, whirling, white robe and borne in the teeth of a roaring norther, Old Man Winter, 1918 model, rolled over the Upland country around the middle of January and for four or five days thereafter, converting stock tanks and water troughs into solid chunks of ice. It plummeted the temperature, Papa figured, by some 90 degrees (an estimate without benefit of thermometer other than Papa's bones and rheumatics, which were, I'd say, 99 per cent accurate). By the time old Model '18 had finished shaking out his mantle, an all-time record of snow had fallen —sixteen to eighteen inches, with drifts higher than the courtyard fence, "and a dang sight higher and dryer than the woodpile," as Papa put it.

The storm had left in its wake two sheepherders frozen to death on King Mountain plus countless poor cows. But the one it really seemed out to get was Fush. And after four or five days it did manage to drive him inside, then to his knees, and finally flat down and clean out of his head with 103–104 degrees fever.

Then was when Papa, generally in the background, moved to the center of the stage. Armed with his primitive, frontier knowledge of medicine plus a package of pink powders and some terse instructions from old Dr. Homer Powers in Rankin, he set in to pull Fush through. Under the best of conditions the picture looked dark. Fush's illness was diagnosed as influenza, the deadly new malady that had already taken three lives in Rankin, and had killed more of our rugged soldier boys than German cannon fire, rifles, and poison gas combined.

"Papa, why don't—why can't Dr. Powers come?" Blanche inquired, tearfully.

"He can't, what with Tom Holland, Elta Windham's husband, and Steve Schnaubert already dead and Ella Schnaubert dyin', and the rest of the town down," Papa said. "So, it's up to you kids and me to pull Fush through."

Shortly, it was up to Papa alone. Blanche, then Gwen, then yours truly went down, but not so seriously ill. So, for the next ten days—and nights—it was touch and go to see who went first, Fush or Old Man Winter. But for Papa's calm, steady nursing, plus the guiding hand of Providence, it would have been Fush. Somehow, from somewhere, Papa summoned something that pulled Fush from the Valley of the Shadow, and got us all back on our feet. With old Brownie, bless her obstinate heart (all the other cows had gone dry), to give enough milk to make the strictly staple diet passably palatable, with Powers pink powders and Papa's perseverance we made it.

Papa's position as county treasurer and his job as sheriff's deputy stood him in good stead in more ways than one. He could keep Fush in the treasurer's office near a steady, coal-burning fireplace. The fact that he left us in the drafty old telephone house, half heated with a potbelly stoked with soggy mesquite, incurred in me no little envy plus an even greater self-pity until Blanche set me straight. "Fush is so much sicker, is why. And besides, Papa is doing this for our own good, since he believes that us being around Fush will make us as sick as he is. Now, just dry up!"

I didn't dry up but I shut up, realizing that Blanche was right. Under guise of intense pain, I did more than my usual quota of crying, part of which was in yearning for Mama, but chiefly through bitterness at her having left us. How I wished for her, but in my more rational moments I took knowledge of her shortcomings in time of crises. Although kind and comforting, not to say pampering in ordinary circumstances, she would be likely to panic in a crisis such as this—turn out to be a hindrance instead of a help and wind up, most likely, another patient.

As a result of Papa's around-the-clock vigilance, pouring in of pink powders and the carrying out of pots, Fush and the rest of us were still around after those two mortal enemies of man, winter and influenza, had been counted out. As was my custom I was ready with questions: "Fush, which you druther have, winter or influenza?" Then it was called by its full, formal, formidable title bespeaking of the deadly potency of it. Not the informal, innocuous "flu" nickname of today, denoting little more than watery eyes and a runny nose.

"I druther not have either one. But I'm happy to tackle the next seventy-five or eighty years ruther than one little bitty case of influenza."

"Fush, I asked Papa, and he said he figures that all that saved your life was them green tomater preserves. Was he a-joshin' me, or not?"

"Yeah, he was a-joshin' you. Fact is, it was them green tomater preserves that nearly killed me in the first place."

"Now, Fush, don't you josh me too. Now . . . "

Here Fush turned serious and set me straight: "No. Honest. The preserves didn't have anything to do with it. Neither did them pink powders. You want to know the only thing saved me? Papa. I was out of my head—*awn concious* as ole Bill would call it—but every time I'd come to, there stood Papa with the mentholatum, the camphor, a turpentine rag, or a coal-oil-and-sugar poultice. Somehow he knew what I needed most each time and he was waitin' there with it—a spoonful of rice, a sip of water, and so on. And when I would come to not needin' or wantin' anything in particular, there stood Papa with just his hand on my forehead.

"Fush, don't you reckon God was there too?"

"Of course God was there too. But, as much as I hate to own up to it, Papa was all I'd look for when I come to. It got to where just before I'd slip away I'd tell myself, "Papa'll be here waitin', expectin' me. *I've got to come back!*" Got off with at having talked so much, Fush tried to close the subject.

"You say Papa was *always* standin' there?"

"Always."

"Then that must have been God that waited on me and Blanche and Gwen. But it looked, acted, and talked exactly like Papa."

"It *was* God. And it was Papa—all rolled into one. It took both of 'em. The shape we was in."

Once the Rankin–Upland road became passable a passing cowboy, one Tex Brightman, brought us news of the latest victim, Ella Schnaubert—her death and burial. Just a few hours before the end her father, a doctor himself, arrived but in spite of all he and Dr. Powers could do she passed on.

Despite the subject matter, and in spite of what we'd been through ourselves, Fush and I couldn't help but be more than somewhat amused at this big, dark-jowled cowboy's manner. Not since the "Taylor, whyn't ye gitche a new saiddleeeeeee?" episode had we been so taken by a narrative style. Not that he had a speech impediment, or a peculiar delivery, or that he was unhandsome like Taylor's *compadre*. Just the opposite. Tex was blessed with a rugged handsomeness plus two rows of the evenest, whitest teeth a girl ever hoped to own. In fact, it was these perfect teeth that put Tex in the Clayburn class (Taylor's *compadre*), for when Tex was relating this tragedy, these striking teeth made him appear as though he was smiling. Yet we knew from the tears in his eyes he wasn't smiling. A second thing that made him stand out in any crowd was that he was a natural cusser. By natural cusser, we mean he could blaspheme without giving offense, for it was plain to one and all that had Tex Brightman realized he was cussing he'd have been the most embarrassed of the crowd. But let's let Tex tell it and see:

"Bygod I hope I never see the likes again. She died, spiter'n hell and two doctors, one her own daddy, leavin' a pore damn little old baby month or two old." Here Tex paused, we thought to wipe the smile off, but to wipe his eyes with a bandanna handkerchief.

"Well, a undertaker or some damn such finally got over from Stockton with a homemade casket—eight or ten of us fellers—all men, not a damn woman in the crowd, laid her on a T-Model with the top down and shoved and sloshed through the meltin' slush out to the graveyard—cold—cold as all hell—and laid her in the grave— grave, hell,—hole not over half deep enough, ground too damn hard. Rocky. No preacher, no nothin' to say a damn prayer over her. God, it was sad."

Once Tex was out of sight and Papa out of earshot, Fush and I unburdened ourselves in unison of what was bearing so heavy on mind, heart, and conscience.

"God, it was sad!"

Then: "Fush, ain't you glad it was pore Ella Schnaubert instead of you, though?"

"Yeah. The dyin' wouldn't a been so bad, but I'd shore hate to have a funeral like Ella's. And most especially, if old Tex preached it."

CHAPTER XXVIII

"Serve Papa right if me and Fush got killed on this trip." I heeled old Babe around savagely and she made a halfhearted lunge, jarring my fancy-banded sailor straw down over my eyes. Just as savagely, I jerked the thing off my head and tried to bust the top out on the saddle horn.

"Wisht Papa had to wear these old straws or eat 'em, one," Fush gritted, sailing his as far as he could send it.

Hats, more than any other article of apparel, reflected a cowboy's ability, or lack of it. And here we were, two cowboys with sailor straws on, about to ride in to Rankin to a picnic. Although we felt that we had outgrown the turtle-tops, we didn't feel mature enough for the sailors.

"Fush, have you ever seen *anybody* wearin' a sailor straw?"

"Not, and 'barefooted,' " he said. "Now I know how Mr. Bishop felt when he saw Solon downtown with a necktie on and barefooted."

"I bet Lee Reynolds wouldn't wear a sailor straw drunk or sober or on a bet," I grumbled.

"Nor Charley Lyons neither," he said, handing me old Polecat's bridle reins. Then he ducked into the house and came out under a miserably battered felt. But at least it had, at one time, showed cowboy styling. I reined old Babe around and refused to untrack, not from shame but from envy. Sorrowfully, he loped out to retrieve the sailor, but doing his best, first, to rein old Polecat onto it. But Polecat, likewise a creature of pride, refused to touch it, even with a hind foot. But Fush wasn't giving up that easy. Ducking into the house once more he shuffled out wearing Blanche's fancy spurs, Apache style, strapped onto his bare heels. The contrast of his extremities was too much. My jag of self-pity gave way to a burst of laughter, hearty and genuine. Fush, strangely enough, wasn't too unhappy all along. Like Papa he could manage somehow on what he had. He was just trying to bring me out of it. Even so, I rode along reveling in past indignities because of un-cowboy apparel, especially hats. And the further I went the more depressed I got; so depressed in fact I reveled in the recalling of the lowest period of my life. Namely, when Mama left, taking Gwen and me with her to Oklahoma.

On the way she had bought me the usual rose-decorated turtle-top straw complete with throat latch like mules wear on blind bridles. At the time it was difficult to determine which had made me the sadder, slipping off from Papa or having to cross Texas in a get-up like that. And me from the cow country. Ordinarily the train ride would have set me delirious with joy, but from the gall of the headgear you'd have thought I was bouncing along in our old wagon. The only flicker of light through the black came at Altus when an Oklahoma whirlwind whisked away that turtle-top, though it almost ended in tragedy. The thing was upon me, almost, before I could loosen the throat latch. Then, the joyful day when Papa came to reclaim Gwen and me was half killed off by another hat worse than the first. For the return trip Papa bought me a little brimless, plaid, cloth hat. Here, I interrupted my reverie to let a bitter, half-smile cross my sneering lips, recalling a just retribution which had befallen Papa on that trip home.

The train was clackety-clacking southwestward at quite a clip with Gwen and me gobbling peanuts by the peck and Papa cutting his Tinsley, a happy smile beaming beneath the brim of the classy

John B. he'd bought in Midland on the way up (the same place, incidentally, he'd bought us these sailor straws).

"Where we at, Papa?" I had asked, a diabolical plot thickening beneath the hated plaid.

"Down around Medicine Mound, I expect. Lemme see." He wrestled a window up and ran his head out. Immediately he jerked it back in, his eyes stricken and the down-grooved corners of his mouth seeping Tinsley.

"My God. My hat's blowed off. Hey, here. Git the porter. Git the brakeman. Git the engineer. Git the president of the Orient road!" He hollered, groping for the bell cord. But he couldn't locate it what with his once-curly hair now hanging, banglike straight down over his eyes.

The train was running late—couldn't stop, but the section gang out of Knox City would pick it up and send it right on.

"What address?"

"Upland. Upland, Texas. Box 25." Then, of course, the man had to know Papa's name, which was more than Papa, in his distraught state, knew for sure.

"J. D. Patterson, cowboy, county treasurer, jailer, fencer, and freighter," I put in, feeling helpful.

With Papa's hair still in his eyes, more or less, I saw my chance and seized it. Loosening my plaid, I stuck my head as far out the window as neck would allow. No business. The thing clung like a cocklebur. I was just fixing to reach up and lend aid when I was jerked violently backward.

"Cut that out, son. I've heard tell of fellers gittin' their heads jerked clean off by bridges." Then Papa's tone softened. "Besides, your hat might blow off." The latter, of course, was my intention; not that I had completely ruled out the former—as a last resort.

While Papa was in the smoker running a comb through his locks, I had seized another opportunity, but the powers were still against me. I was sorely tempted to reach up and wipe the thing off, but fear of a tattletale aboard—here I had cut an eye at Gwen—I commenced to resort to the insidious method of making my scalp crawl. This made the thing leech on all the tighter. Jerking my head back inside I pouted for a hundred miles. "Sweetwater, next stop," galvanized me into action. Papa, now considering himself stark naked, would be getting off in Sweetwater to buy himself another hat. So maybe if . . . , he'd buy me one like his. Here I wouldn't even let my thoughts form the scheme in mind. But what with Papa scootching down now as far out of sight as possible he wasn't likely to see me.

Throwing caution to the winds—where I hoped the plaid would soon be—I slapped it on the window sill. Three times it teetered and fell back inside. Then was when I hauled off and pitched it out. As if in a vision an airtight alibi came to me. I was just reaching over to let Papa have same when I felt a hand on my arm. It was a kid from three windows back. He handed me my little plaid hat. And the dirty scoundrel must have been thirteen years old, thus rendering my rage impotent. My next pouting spell lasted to Midland. Here I was almost as ashamed of Papa as I was of myself. His hat had blown off and mine hadn't. Shame had switched to high dander, however, when . . . .

"Paul, wake up and ride like a cowboy. Here's Rankin. You've been dreamin' along there for a hour."

"Out of the nightmare into the fire," I mumbled to myself, kicking old Babe as if it were her fault. Then: "Fush, I don't see why Sog laughs about Mr. Bishop wearin' his hat in the house and sleepin' in it. I would too if I had me a John B."

"Me too," said Fush, jingling his spurs.

"Barefooted and spurs on. Fush, take them things off. Bad enough, these old straws . . . ."

Fush not only complied, but he removed the straw and tucked it under his arm.

We rode into Rankin feeling like two coyotes slipping up on a hen house. Anchoring our mounts at a hitch rack we took it afoot, hoping, for once, to pass as town dudes. As luck would have it, we encountered not a single kid citizen on the street. Neither were there any in Felps & Taylor's store. Nobody in, at the moment, except Pappy Taylor, and he was just like home folks. Everybody else out at the barbecue, where we'd be, but for the hats.

Dinner bought and straws stashed at a safe distance away, so that they could just as well be taken for part of the merchandise, we sort of hoped some of the Rankin boys would happen in. For here is where we felt we shined—eating out. Thanks to Papa's careful teaching and proper eating example we did it just like they did in Fort Worth and other places. Fush ordered the usual—box of saltines, cut of cheese, and two cans of sardines.

"And a can of tomaters for dessert," right out of a clear sky. Nothing chinchy about us, I thought, swelling with pride momentarily. Then my heart sank. Since tomatoes (fancies) never were on Papa's menu, how does a man go about eating them proper?

"Watch me, is all." Fush said, reading my anxious eye.

Moving to the back of the "staple and fancy" counter we proceeded to eat as politely and as properly as Papa had taught us to do on a couple of previous trips—stabbing out the sardines with our pocket knives (never with the fingers) and taking them directly off the blade with the mouth. Though I never made a bobble, Fush said later, it proved rather awkward for me, having to switch from the left hand. But Fush said Papa had said it would have been ill-mannered otherwise. The dessert, as it turned out, was eaten same as the main course, with the knife. When we got outside we called it *"desert"* like Herman Jackson did, though we wouldn't have dared in Mr. Taylor's presence (for fear of being taken for "hicks.") We had a good laugh about that.

"Fush, old Herman shore ain't been around much, has he?"

"Shore ain't."

Somewhat self-assured, after our seeming success at eating we claimed our straws (reluctantly) and went out to the barbecue in search of companionship. As soon as they recovered from the shock of the sailors, the Rankin boys, to our partial relief, took us to their collective hearts. What won them was the skill with which Fush could sail that sailor. He could cut a chicken's throat at thirty paces with the sharp edge of it. What's more, he would toss it under any passing cowboy's skittish bronc or lend it to any other kid with the nerve to do likewise.

Not as quick to mix—or to forget—I poked along behind the others, hat under arm and brooding deeply over the indignity of a cowboy having to appear in public under such a monstrosity. Now and then I'd fling the thing at a passing auto, praying it would land underneath a wheel.

The debut of these straws was also their final public appearance. We plucked a couple of staves out of the JM fence and played polo as far back toward home as they lasted. By the time we reined up at our little corral gate there wasn't enough straw left to make a humming bird's nest.

CHAPTER XXIX

"We're movin'," Papa announced, right out of the clear blue early September sky. Even though Papa was saying it for the thirtieth time it came as a terrific shock, to Blanche more than to the rest of us even though she had heard it nearly twice as many times. And she expressed our sentiments exactly:

"But, Papa, we like it fine right here at Upland."

"Upland is played out, Peggy. Blowed up. What the drouth didn't dry out, last winter's blizzard froze out. Cowmen all broke. Nothin' to freight, no grass to fence around, no work to be had. Got to go where the work's at."

"Where'll that be?"

"Down the country a-ways. East."

"Where down the country a-ways?" Blanche was big enough now to express herself rather bluntly at times. And she was on solid ground here, realizing she had Papa on the defensive.

"Down towards Ranger. The oil fields. But if our money runs too short we'll have to stop off on some farm or another and work awhile."

"Some farm?"

"Some farm?"

"Some farm?" This came from Blanche right on down to me, each voice progressively higher, in dismay.

"But, Papa, I can't stand old flat farmin' land. Too ugly."

"A bellyful is better'n a eyeful."

"What does that mean, Papa?" This from Gwen, now on the threshold of a voiced curiosity. But Papa, now at the threshold of voiced exasperation, ruled further questions and rebuttals irrelevant, and, capable disciplinarian though he was, he couldn't discipline the unvoiced.

"We went through that country on the train, Fush," I whispered, "not a cowboy in a thousand miles. Besides, we can't ever again ride in the Reed Buick."

"Can't anyhow, unless Alvin finds that Castle Gap gold. Or somethin'.

"He might, at that." I said, brightening perceptibly. Then I realized we wouldn't be here to enjoy it.

"Wisht Sog was here, maybe he could stop Papa."

"Nah. He's gone down there hisself. Remember? One reason Papa's headed that-a-way."

"Wasn't Sog, but Ralph, that started it all," I said, bitter at Ralph even if he was my own brother. He had left Granddad Pollard's and had tolled Sog away from the JM's to the Ranger-Breckenridge boom. Just when Sog was beginning to come home on raw broncs and with shop-made boots on. *Goodbye, Cowboy*!

Papa, his ear deaf and head set, commenced readying the old prairie schooner for number *thirty*. Covered wagons at their very classiest were almost extinct, so this one with homemade square top proved too much for Blanche to face.

"Papa, I refuse to set foot in that ridiculous, silly thing," Blanche said, almost in tears.

"I didn't expect you to, Peggy," Papa said, "I was aimin' to send you up to your Aunt Zo's till we got settled somewhere."

That still left me and Fush to ride in the thing. (Gwen didn't count. She would ride with Papa in anything to anywhere, anytime.) To us this square-top thing was as galling as the sailor straws. Even more so, for, in case of a whirlwind one could quietly dispose of a sailor straw. But Papa still wasn't much for show, still wasn't one to live one copper cent beyond his means. Give him a makeshift, pot-bedecked, stovepipe-strung covered wagon with homemade bows of his own any day, rather than a brand new Cole 8 on credit.

"It's what a feller has got on the inside; not what he looks like he has got on the outside," was Papa's line of defense, when we crowded him, which we didn't anymore now that our leader, Blanche, was gone on to Aunt Zo's. And as Sog had put it so long ago and so aptly: "If you think you're changin' Papa any, you're jist mooin' at the moon."

Sad farewells said to the Reeds and to Upland, we boarded that scarecrow schooner and rolled east. For once we were thankful for Papa's early rising and quick starting. Under cover of darkness we would be spared the humiliation of being seen in this ridiculous vehicle, and almost as important, we would avoid seeing our beloved Upland fade out behind us forever.

Come daylight I sneaked as far back inside the schooner as I could with Fush and old Philip ranging as far away as possible. Now and then, however, the old dog would condescend to trot along in the vehicle's shade to cool off. Even then he didn't have the heart to look anybody in the eye. Only Whitey, true daughter of a jackass, and Papa were without shame, not seeming to care who might be watching.

"Somethin's up," said Fush.

Something *was* up, but we were too occupied to fathom what it was. Only after the last two crackers, cemented together with peanut butter, had gone down the hatch, and power of speech recovered did we commence to analyze Papa's peculiar behavior. By now he had pulled off the main road and was headed south.

"Ain't we a-goin' to Ranger, Papa?" Fush asked, startled.

Papa shook his head in the negative, his mouth too occupied with Tinsley to voice even the word "no."

"Why not?" Ordinarily Fush's tone of voice would have brought him his comeuppance. But Papa, strangely tolerant, merely bathed a double tree in Tinsley juice and explained:

"Old ponies played out. Horse feed's played out. Money's played out. Even our luck was played out—till I got us this little maize-headin' contract down the road here a-ways."

"On a farm?"

"On a farm?"

"On a farm?"

Contract? On a farm?. Contracts in the cow country had spelled disaster. Contracts in the clodhopper country would spell calamity plus. Consequently questions in a tone of voice that, ordinarily, in Papa's eyes would have bordered on insubordination if not outright insurrection. But here he remained calm, even solicitous.

"Got to get you kids somewheres so's you can thaw out and dry out. You want to mildew?"

"Not on no farm, we don't."

From the sudden hardening of Papa's eye and the lumping of his jaw muscles Gwen and I thought better of seconding Fush this time. But those were our sentiments exactly.

CHAPTER XXX

The eighth sunup out of Upland, justification for brooding was increased a hundredfold but with time to do it decreasing proportionately. Fush and I were plodding drearily, wearily behind Papa who was, in turn, plodding behind an ancient, asthmatic gray mule drawing a sled between two rows of grain. We were heading maize. *Beheading* would have been a more apt description, for I could visualize in mind's eye every head that fell under the knife as that of old Dutch, our employer.

Two noble cowboys reduced to this. Everything dear in this life behind us—big country, wild cattle, wild cowboys, good horses. Nothing ahead but a wheezy, staggery gray mule and jillions of itchy, scratchy heads of maize. Chafed by the unaccustomed steady labor, chafed to the point of distraction by maize chaff down our necks from sun to sun, we felt that we had reached the ultimate of chafings. But we had known absolutely nothing about chafings until we learned of the designs old Dutch had on the Claude Harrell filly.

"When the old ――― led his pore old blind mother in and introduced her to Papa I should have warned him then," Fush said. He didn't say the name out loud, but may as well have, from the shape of his lips.

As a concession (so he thought) to us Papa let us ride old Heave

Ho back to the house at quitting time. Since Papa cut straight through and we went around by the gate we took all sorts of liberties with the despised beast. To trigger one of his smothering spells we would tighten his throat latch and lash him into a brisk trot. Then when he took down with a wheezing, staggering seizure, one of us would take up the throat latch another notch. But old Heave turned out to be set up of stern and stable stuff indeed. Distemper, disease, plus the diabolical doings of cruel young masters, succeeded only in bringing him to his knees occasionally. His recoveries became as chafing as maize chaff down the neck.

"I've heard of people not dyin', just turnin' into a gray mule," Fush said. "Looks like the case here. Old Dutch's Papa, most likely."

These slurs old Heave was pondering in his black heart. Come unhitching time he would get in his licks and kicks. Being foolish about his ears, he was hazardous to the nth degree at unbridling time. A sweep of his anvilhard head was most as lethal as a lick from the other end. A couple of times each evening he would rap Fush so hard against the fence you could hear the *bois d'arc* posts groan. That very first evening Fush had grabbed up a cedar stave and was fixing to wield it when something prompted him to glance toward the house. It was, unfortunately, too close for brash deeds and words.

"Whoahhhhhhh, you ol' ———," Fush hollered. "Wisht I was Papa for half a second. I'd call you what you are."

"If I was Papa I would cut his d——*ng* throat," I reminded him, hard put to stay even one letter away from outright profanity.

Blanche's appearance on the scene brightened our outlooks, though only momentarily. Even a 100 per cent improvement in the quality of the cooking wasn't enough to lift us from the slough of despond. Neither was the great quantity of fancies enough to cheer us. Give me out west even on cornbread and molasses. Our sagging spirits were again bolstered (mine only slightly and fleetingly) by the return of Sog and Ralph to the fold. This meant that now we would not be released from bondage since our original destination was their oil-field headquarters.

Come daylight next morning the five of us were plodding behind old Heave. From the corner of a jaundiced eye I studied Ralph and Sog to see how long it would take them to crack, to crumble, to fall to staves like a dry barrel. But here was a cross they seemed to be bearing very well, in fact disgustingly well, considering the fact that they had both been cowboys. I actually believe they were deriving satisfaction from this miserable occupation—maybe actual pleasure. Like a crazy fool Bailey Foster told us about being whipped with blacksnakes and trace chains. And this dangerous state of mind soon seized hold of Fush, leaving me to rail and rant alone against the adversities of Fate, to hold high the bandanna banner of the cowboy.

This constant railing against the slings and arrows of outraged fortune seemed to drive a wedge between me and Fush. In fact, it brought about a rift between me and all my brothers—a sort of a modern day parallel of Joseph and *his* cruel brothers. Physically, they never laid a hand on me, even in self-defense. Their persecutions were more insidious, more intolerable than physical violence. And so subtle! Their method of meting out torture was to jot down, during the course of my railings, my many mispronunciations, misinterpretations, and malapropisms. Then in the dead hours of the night they would waken me from a deep, sweet sleep and sing back my sayings in verses they had composed and set to what they called *music*.

Just because I found the sowbelly "ransome," the "round rod" hung in the barrel of the .22, the sun "red and hot," old Philip "layin' around the ground, this trio felt compelled to set same to song with which to serenade me nightly:

> Paul got up and looked in the pot
> And says I want my "ransome" crow
> Good and red and hot.

Then, following a bouquet of brogans, boots, and bootjacks they would bow in for the encore:

> Paul got up and looked on the shelf
> And says I want the "round rod" all to myself.

Malapropisms exhausted, they turned to my common complaints and laments for fresh material, especially the ones I employed at getting-up time (or rather at three hours previous to getting-up time, at which hour we arose):

> Paul got up a-lookin' mighty sour
> And says "tell Papa I haven't slept a hour."

> Paul got up and buckled up his belt
> And says I wisht Papa *knowed* how I felt.

They knew I knew better than to use *knowed*. They also knew it to be a better way to stir me to the very depths of my being. Finally the closing verse, if and when Papa didn't close the show prematurely:

> Paul went out and whistled to his hound;
> Purty soon he found him layin' "around the ground."

There should have been another verse about my fondness for vanilla wafers—which I pronounced "wawfers." This was their pronunciation also, hence no verse. I continue to speculate, after fifty years, how they could have composed such a verse, but they could have. And it would have rhymed.

Maize chaff, heat, drudgery, and old Heave Ho notwithstanding, the days were becoming less dreaded than the nights. A constant and compulsive talker by day, I brooked no interference. Nor did I heed interruptions. Only at the dinner table were they able to wedge a word in edgeways now and then. But powerful words they were, and maddening to the extreme, but so subtly put and so delicately accented that Papa didn't see how he could take issue:

RALPH: Paul Patters-on.

SOG: Yes, Paul Patters on. And on.

FUSH: Indeed yes, Paul Patters on. AND ON. AND ON!"

ME: "Papa, make them . . . "

"We apologize, Papa. Paul's a good kid, Paul is. Now, he may not look it. But he is *so human*." This from Ralph, of course, whom Papa didn't quite know how to cope with. In fact there wasn't any way for Papa to cope with the situation, so at the first opportunity he coached me on how to cope with it. Tonight when this troublesome trio got up to sing, I would join them. Make it a quartet. Astounding! After a couple of stanzas you would have thought that this quartet (three of them, that is) were singing at their own funeral.

The *coup de grace* to their heckling, however, came from a couplet of my own composition, which I sang as a solo:

> Paul got up and started in to bawl
> And says tell Papa I haven't slep' at all!

All together now:

> Paul got up and started in to bawl
> And says tell Papa I haven't slep' at all!

But the encore was a straight out solo as well. Their stricken faces told me that they were whipped, through, finished. At least for the night.

As I suspected, next day at dinner they made their final, desperate bid. They resuscitated an old one that had always set me to throwing cookware. Bolting their food, the three, at spaced intervals, jumped up and left the table:

"Paul eats a heap."

"Paul does eat a heap."

"Paul eats a heapin' heap."

Pushing my own plate back I stood up and cleared my throat for attention:

Ralph and Sog and Fush kep' talkin' in their sleep;
All they kep' a-sayin' was "Paul eats a heap."

The rhyme was more than commonplace, the tune was terrible but this baffling behavior finished them, as a trio at least, for some time to come. Even so they would have continued their heckling ways but for the fact that there was unearthed for them a brand new straight man, fall guy, or joke butt. But it was no joking matter. And, luckily for old Dutch, they came upon this bit of intelligence after the maize crop was laid by. Otherwise the last head that fell in the sled would have been Dutch's. Ralph had found out that Papa had contracted this twelve acres of maize at $3.00 an acre, a contract that took five Pattersons thirty days (measured by suns) to fulfill. By Sog's computing that amounted to $1.20 per day or nearly 25 cents apiece—around two cents per man-hour.

"In that case," put in Ralph, still reluctant to give up the heckling, "I think it only fair for Paul to turn his two cents worth back to poor ol' Dutch." This out of earshot of Papa. Hoorawing was one thing; rubbing it in was another. This was how Papa was. Never had been and never could be otherwise. Honest as the day was long, and as willing as ever came down the pike. But completely helpless, hopeless, when it came to dealing, especially with the likes of old Dutch. Just how hopelessly helpless he was in Dutch's clutches, was shortly to strike us with the impact of Heave Ho's hind hoofs square in the belly.

CHAPTER XXXI

Maize crop laid by we were fixing to set in on the cotton patch when we got wind of a disagreement between Papa and old Dutch. They couldn't come to terms on how much we should be paid a hundred.

"Couldn't come to terms with Papa?" Sog said, his lower jaw bouncing off his brisket. "Somethin' fishy here. This rain musta mildewed Papa's mind."

"Sog's right. We better get a-hold of Papa and get the hell outta here," Ralph said, big enough to cuss and glad of it.

"Goodbye, Broadway, hello, France," sang Blanche, fox-trotting across the room.

"Goodby *thirty*, hello, *thirty-one*, you mean," sang Fush.

"Hallelujah, born again!" I yelled.

"I repeat, let's find Papa and get the hell outta here," said Ralph, his salty suggestion galvanizing us into action. When we found Papa in the barn patching harness we felt that Sog's fears of fishiness were well founded. Papa acted like somebody harboring some dark secret in his heart, a secret he was loathe to let go of. Whatever it was it was something sacred, something precious, say, like a virgin's virginity. Then, like Zen Buddhism it was revealed to us in one bright, galvanic flash: that verminous villain Dutch Porter had violated our virgin! To what extent we had no way of knowing until we had hooked up and pulled out.

Too blinded by tears and rage, I couldn't see to what extent until the schooner was well out to sea, east bound. Babe, thank the Lord, was still amongst us. But in the harness with her was a high-eared, hard-tailed half-horse, half-ass. The hated Heave Ho! If this was a blow I hadn't felt anything yet. Through flowing tears and falling rain I searched for the others. Not a trace. The beloved black mare, the most beloved Whitey, the trim Claude Harrell filly—all gone.

"Oh, Lord. Old Philip too?" I was fixing to scream when my nose caught wind of him, sloshing along under the wagon.

"Just two mares and a burro, Papa? Couldn't you have throwed in Paul?" Ralph, of course.

Papa's answer, if any, was drowned in my (and Gwen's) tears, with accompanying sound effects.

"What kind of boot did you get?" This from Sog, which answer, if any, was crowded out by Fush's aside to me.

"I know what kind of boot he oughta got—a box-toed one square in the butt."

"Never see ol' Whitey again in this world. Booooo ahhhhhh," I wailed.

"No, but you can look at it this way," Ralph whispered his condolences. "You won't see that son of a bitchin' Dutch again either."

"If I ever do," Fush put in, "I hope it's down the sights of a thirty-thirty. Ol' crook thinks he's one smart *hombre*. And maybe he is. But he better thank his stars for a blind mother and a peg-legged brother, she a-gropin' and he a-limpin' in and out. They're what closed the deal for him."

Here a deep bitterness, a rankling resentment assailed me, a goodly portion of it aimed at Papa. All right to pity a poor old blind woman and a one-legged man. But how about his own kids? How could he do such a cruel thing to us? Only the years were able to clear up that question. Though the exact terms of the trade will remain locked in the breasts of Papa and old Dutch, we were able to ferret out Papa's reasons: Because of poor contracting ability, and the incessant rain as its ally, he was forced to make the swap, with some to boot, to make ends meet and pay his bills. Too, he wanted a bit left over for a rainy day. But with every day rainy, what else was an honest man to do?

CHAPTER XXXII

Thirty-one turned out to be a shotgun shack two miles from Roscoe and a half mile off the Sweetwater road. Twenty-four hours on these cotton patch premises was enough to implant in my bosom a burning yearning for *thirty-two*. Maize-heading, which a man had to do on foot, was low enough. But with cotton picking he had to get clear down on his knees thirteen hours at a stretch, except for the sowbelly sandwich break around noontime. To the others, as far as I could tell, it was just another job. But to me it was another sentence. As it turned out, my sentiments were also those of Ralph who was brash enough to express same. But, whereas I hated the long hours and short rations *per se*, he resented only the confinement of it.

Once the cotton was picked and Papa had landed a grubbing contract Ralph had begun to suffer severe seizures of the "go yonders." (Meantime we had achieved *thirty-two*—from Mr. Wade's cotton-patch shack to a Mr. Philips' mesquite-flat shanty hard by the T & P Railroad.) Severe as Ralph's seizure proved to be, he was soonered by Blanche's visiting cowboy friend, Henry Kaiser. Not for love nor money would Henry grub stumps any longer. However, he assured Blanche that it was lack of *money* that was driving him off. (A logical conclusion since Papa had contracted the land-clearing project at $1.25 per acre.) So, selling Papa the Double X

Black and bidding Blanche a sad adieu he sacked his saddle and caught the westbound Sunset Limited.

Shortly thereafter Ralph defected. He had grubbed and grunted and strained half a day on one stump about the size of a "Peter Schuttler wagon loaded with broom corn" (his description), then another hour or so gnawing a keg-size taproot in two with his double-bitted (two bit) ax. Burying the blade in the fork of the next mesquite to be felled he turned to Papa and said, "Papa, I have done made my dime for today, so I *do* believe I will quit while I am ahead."

Regardless of how Ralph worded a pronouncement he had a way of making it go down easy. In fact it was a very diplomatic way of easing out, so the measly $1.25 per acre wouldn't be spread so thin. It wouldn't go too far with postwartime bacon $3 to $4 a side, and not much cheaper from the belly. At $2.00 a hundred that fall in the cotton patch, the combined Patterson income had totaled as high as $23.40 in a single day. That was incredible and beyond our wildest dreams, but because of the exceptionally rainy year only one or two days out of six could be devoted to cotton picking—though *devoted* is not quite the term for it. Even so, a far cry from the piddling pittance Papa had contracted this job for.

Calling Sog aside Ralph tried to rescue him from such a fate. No go.

"You mean you will keep on a-grubbin'?"

"Why not. It beats workin'."

By suppertime Ralph had pulled out, figuring that one meal (after that stump) would be crowding Papa's profit margin too close. He was right. Just as anticipated quietly and behind hands, the grubbing contract succeeded only in yielding appetites bigger than profits.

"Nothin' makes grub disappear faster than grubbin'," philosophized the philosopher.

Another couple of months, the last thirty days of which was steady rain, and Papa was ready to holler "calf rope." It wasn't the first part—twelve hours a day at the end of an ax or grubbing-hoe handle that got him. It was the idleness—all outgo and no income. With Blanche in the kitchen full time, and not in the cotton patch where she could pick circles around the whole outfit, the outgo exceeded the income by a frightening margin.

Fush, even, was fairly good at homework—reading saddle catalogs—on exceptionally bad days.

"I'm orderin' me a fish brand slicker," he said, "I can't stand this another day. I druther be goin' to school, even."

"And fight them mean kids?" I asked it before I thought.

"At least it's somethin' to do."

Eventually even I had had a bellyful of rainwater. So it was with joyful hearts that we heard Papa propose another move. This joy, needless to say, was tempered with anxiety until we wrung from Papa the direction.

"Which-a-way?"

"West," he said, evoking five sighs of relief.

"Where at?"

"Place called Balmorhea."

"How far?"

"Two hundred and fifty miles, I expect. Maybe more."

"*Exactly where* is Balmorhea?" Blanche only, what with Papa having neared his answer quota for the day.

"Right smart ways west of Upland," said Papa, still not what you would call pinpointing our destination, but no sense crowding our luck, which was already straining at the stakerope.

"Let's see, now," Sog said, "accordin' to my figures—twenty-nine plus four (carry your one) this would make old *thirty-three* comin' up. Well, thirty-third time's the charm."

Or was it? That very night, something besides our luck strained at the stakerope and succeeded in breaking loose—our work team was boogered by a train, and old Babe had vanished, vamoosed. Papa picked up her trail and followed it for ten miles afoot, but when dark overtook him he lost it and had to turn back. Just as old

Whitey had been, Babe was one of the family and just *had* to be found. Too, I wanted to shake the mud of that cursed place from my feet and be long gone before another maize-heading, cotton-picking, grubbing season rolled around.

I must interpolate here to say that Papa, under the wary and watchful eye of both Sog and Ralph (who had reappeared once the coast—and the mesquite stumps—were cleared), had driven in to Sweetwater and swapped the Double X Black for old Nell, a seven-year-old gray mare of Babe's conformation and disposition. And what is more incredible still, had neither blot nor blemish of physique or psyche.

"No boot nor nothin'?" Fush asked in a skeptical aside to Sog.

"No boot nor nothin'. Beat anything ever I seen. Papa was something to behold."

"You haf to give the other feller some credit," Ralph put in, "for not havin' come out leadin' his blind old mother or a afflicted child."

"A kid with a bad cold you mean," Sog put in, then repeated, "Honest to God. Papa was mag*nif*icent."

Magnificent or no, they didn't dare let him out of their sight from that day forward. Every time he hooked Nell to a borrowed buggy and went on a scout for Babe, one of them would chaperone him.

Sending Blanche and Gwen to Aunt Zo's, Papa and the big boys scouted as far west as Colorado City and south into the Champion community. And a couple of times they checked back with Old Dutch at Loraine. But he hadn't seen hair nor hide of her. He claimed.

"Did you all look in the old son of a ———," Fush paused and glanced at Papa, judging his distance. Not willing to take the risk he finished decently—"gun's barn?"

"No. A slick horsethief like Dutch'd leave her with some crony. Till we left the country."

But for a proneness to chronic hunger—and bawling spells—I'd have preferred being with Babe, wherever she was. But life in camp wasn't turning out so bad. What with store-boughten wagon bows and a brand new wagon sheet—some of Blanche's frills—we were "rug bug snug." Also, because of our proximity to the railroad tracks, Papa's cooking attracted as fascinating a clientele as Fush and I ever popped an eye at. However coarse its fare, Patterson hospitality was of the finest. Hobos were always welcome to a handout, such as it was.

"You fellers ought to can stand it if we can," was Papa's stock invitation, which got as monotonous to Fush and me as the grub did. These fellows with their crisp, precise accents sounded like gentlemen of culture, and deserved something more original—and appetizing. Gentlemen they were too in that they never infringed upon our hospitality or swiped so much as a crust of flapjack.

Papa marveled at the fact that so few of them hit us up, having heard that bums leave certain marks indicating the easy marks.

"I don't believe they pass the word on," he said.

"Maybe they *do* is why," said Sog.

CHAPTER XXXIII

Fush had long since begun to fret and fume, but I was completely content with this jolly, carefree life with bums. By now the straying Babe had diminished from a major calamity to a mere incident. However, a bit of intelligence passed down from Sog moved it back into the calamity class—or above.

"Unless we find a job of work pretty quick, Papa says he's gonna take a city scavenger job."

"City scavenger? Here?" I asked, seized by a severe anxiety state.

"Not so loud," Fush cautioned, glancing uneasily toward the bums huddled over the morning stew. "You wanta lose the last friends we got?"

"Here?" I asked again, careful not to repeat the term "scavenger." In those days there was no hiding behind high-sounding terms.

"No. Loraine," he whispered.

Loraine. As from Job, the word wrung from me an exceeding loud bitter cry, plus thoughts of equal bitterness—*back in the cunning clutches of Dutch*, quite possibly the purloining of Babe and Nell, maybe more maize heading, and so on. Here I found myself ransacking the memory for a verse of scripture or a prayer whereby I could take my burdens to the Lord and leave them there.

Nothing. Nothing at all save the bitterness, much of which I directed toward my own self. What I get for paying more attention to Granddad's vittles than I had his blessings.

Communication cut off from the Lord, I could have gone to Papa but avoided it like a plague, preferring to hang onto the feeble thread of a possibility that Sog was hurrawing us. Yet in my heart I knew the naked, brutal truth. For Papa no work was too mean—too menial—as long as it was honest.

City scavenger. Heretofore, the term had always brought a laugh. But this close to home it was a topic not to be touched upon, even in the presence of bums. "Beggars can't be choosers." No? But they can be mighty choicy about jobs. And about friends who are not, I thought, torn between envy and resentment. Deep in the slough of despond I awaited the outcome like a hospital patient overhearing the doctor pronounce his case "terminal." Fush, on the other hand, took a keener interest in hoboing instructions— how to hop a freight properly, how to ride the blinds, how to dodge the railroad bulls. Papa might turn scavenger but Fush harbored higher aspirations.

Eventually the scales tipped—though almost imperceptibly—in our favor. Right after Papa had bought a hip-sprung nag to fill Babe's harness she was found. The seller, a rare breed of horse trader indeed, refunded Papa's money and took the horse back.

Babe turned up in a farmer's lot not far from old Dutch's domain. She wore no brand—nobody in the Patterson household with the heart to stick a hot iron to Babe. From what Papa could piece together, Dutch knew she was there all the time; he was keeping quiet until we left and then he would claim her. He had practically stolen the others, why not Babe too? Since horse-thief hanging was already out of favor, except among us kids, we couldn't get Papa to push it. He had neither the money nor the time, which turned out a blessing in disguise, after all. Suddenly we recalled the city scavenger menace and wouldn't have laid over another twelve hours even for a hanging.

"Unless," Fush pointed out later, "it was a double hangin'—old Dutch and the old feller that might offer Papa the scavenger job."

"Papa, hadn't we better take roundants on Loraine? Ain't it a mighty sandy pull for these old 'clivises'?" I suggested subtly, using Papa's own expression in a further effort to sway him.

"No, I reckon not," Papa said, settling that part of it. As for myself I remained unsettled and extremely so until well west of Loraine, after which crisis I leapt from the schooner and hit the ground running—to join Fush and old Philip at their positions as flank scouts.

"Another narrow one behind us, Fush, Thank God A'mighty." I was hard put to keep from yelling it but Papa frowned on the use of anything stronger than "golleee bum" for a nine year old. And even the "bum" had been ruled out lately, lest we offend our guests.

"By the skin of our ——— teeth." Fush said, repressing just in the nick, another forbidden word. After all, with Loraine just a couple of sand dunes back, no sense in tempting fate.

"Man born of woman is of few days and full of trouble." The gloating over the Loraine thing and glorying in the prodigal mare's return was shortly to be smothered by the sudden and tragic passing of old Philip. Between Colorado City and Iatan he was trotting along minding his own business when some high-toned smart alec ran him down in an automobile. The fact that it was a hit-and-run driver was all that saved his being torn limb from limb. I would still love automobiles but I would never again trust an auto driver. Auto driving, I decided, must make a man lose respect for dogs.

We buried brave, beloved old Philip a good ways from the road, so his grave wouldn't be violated and defiled by some debased motorist. We were somewhat consoled by the fact that it was excellent rabbit country. And Papa, after a fashion, had preached him a moving funeral, touching and poetic, which wasn't like Papa except in its brevity:

He's gone where the woodbine twineth
And the peckerwood mourneth.

But for the fact that we were headed back to cow country—
and still too close to scavengerless Loraine—we'd have mourned by
his graveside a few days and guarded it against coyotes, auto drivers
and other varmints.

CHAPTER XXXIV

Papa, in a gesture calculated to lessen the burden of our grief, made the following announcement: "A right smart out of our way but we'll swing by your Aunt Zo's for a few days."

A bighearted gesture notwithstanding, it brought on another of my anxiety states. Time was I would have greeted Papa's announcement with great rejoicing, but at that time we had owned a fairly respectable hack, when hacks weren't too many years behind the times; but now this covered wagon (even with its brand new bows and sheet) was as outmoded as prisoner's stocks and twice as humiliating. And it did look slightly ridiculous parked alongside their Cole 8 automobile. Besides, my clothes weren't fit for such an occasion. Worse yet I was suffering from a most embarrassing malady. I didn't know the medical term for it but in layman's lingo it was the cotton picker's itch. In those brutal old days of calling a spade a spade they couldn't—or wouldn't—dodge behind false labels.

The others, through perseverance, persistence, self-discipline and nightly number-2 tubs of sulphur water, had cured themselves. And they thought they had seen to it that I had done likewise. Feigning extreme modesty, bolstered by outcries of outrage, I had taken advantage of their absence from the room and managed to bypass these baths. For reasons known only to modern psychiatry I preferred scratching to scrubbing, itching to washing. Now my sins were sure to find me out what with thrice the number of relatives around to observe. I wasn't kidding myself that sleeping at the foot of the bed would offer me any more privacy.

The moment we disembarked upon Aunt Zo's premises my malady would become quite obvious, if it itched with its usual intensity. Besides, certain areas of the affected regions showed through my threadbare clothes. To add insult to discomfort there would be the covered wagon. Blanche, Gwen, and Sog had gotten to make the trip by train thus leaving the brunt of this thing on the frail shoulders of Fush and me. Papa, of course, didn't count, inured as he was to shame of any sort (as evidenced by the scavenger application). Besides, he managed to stay fairly well dressed —on either end, at least.

A half day short of Aunt Zo's we stopped in at the sand-locked village of Coahoma for haircuts. Heartened at the chance to add to my appearance I quit the wagon with too much eagerness. From the draft aft I realized that the brake handle had raked away the seat of my pants, leaving me on the horns of a dilemma. Should I report the seatless condition of my last pair of pants and maybe risk Papa's applying a switch direct? Or should I let it ride and take my chances on concealing the whole thing? I'd let it ride. As regards my chances of concealing the whole thing? They were good, with Fush around to act as rear guard. But what if I should need Fush to front for me, to face a situation too formidable for me, such as, right now, the braving of this barber. And as regards said situation I so stated.

"Okay, then, turn around and back in."

"Don't tease me, Fushhhhhhhh."

Though he continued to tease me, not with words but with eye movements, facial expressions, and deaf-and-dumb finger signs we'd gotten from our first reader, he shielded my bare seat making it possible for me to beat a discreet retreat.

While Fush scouted the sandhills, I stayed in the schooner, desperately searching for pleasant memories of our last visit to drown out dread of the impending one. Fortunately, of pleasant memories there were plenty, for example, my second moving picture, western at that, in the very theater where our cousin, Viv, played the mood and background music. How beyond one's wildest dreams much less beyond *Thirty-one Years on the Plains and in the Mountains*, to sit in on a scalping set to music—music played by one's own flesh and blood! "That's my cousin a-playin' the peanna," I had confided to everyone within earshot, which was quite a crowd back in those silent movie days.

Vivid likewise were the magnificent meals—a far cry from sowbelly, sorghum and, lately, Karo. Then there was the imposing mansion of seven or eight gables, the gorgeous furniture, the thick carpets, the shiny floors, the wide, imposing staircase whose steps led directly up to the pearly gates—and possibly beyond. Finally, and mainly, there was the great, sleek, shiny Cole 8 automobile.

And there was the kind, generous concern of Aunt Zo, the beauty, talent, and graciousness of the three girls, the congenial affability of the two boys. And, lastly, the gruff, railroad-man cordiality of Uncle Pete, a kindly man in spite of his admonition to Fush and me to "try to keep your hands off the wallpaper." After all, how was he to know we couldn't stand up on those ice-slick floors without support.

Reassuring reminiscences to be sure but always rising up to crowd out this pleasant past was this specter of the grim present and ominous future. Namely, a wagon whose top was covered and a child whose bottom wasn't.

CHAPTER XXXV

With an ear-busting clank of iron wheels and a tinkle of trace chains, Papa wheeled into the gravel driveway and pulled up abreast of a sleek Cole 8.

"Ho, girls," he hollered, sawing back on the lines.

"Ho, girls," he yelled again, as Blanche, Gwen, Aunt Zo, and girls answered from the back porch. They came bounding out to meet us as if we'd just rolled up in a Cadillac. And from Papa's mien and manner—his air of assurance—you'd think we had. Wrap hitching the lines on a wheel hub he kissed everybody and started to hand down Fush and me. Fush, bumfuzzled at Papa's peculiar concern, jumped by him. But I stayed in my tree, postponing as long as possible my true state of affairs.

"Come on down, Paul, honey. Aren't you glad to see us?" Aunt Zo said, holding out her arms.

"Why. Yes, ma'am. I'm puttin' on my shoes." (I hadn't had them off since Roscoe, five nights ago.)

Exhausting every stall and subterfuge I finally had to hop down into Aunt Zo's arms, then to Blanche's then to Mary's then to Viv's, and so on. Finally, there was little Gwen whom I scarcely recognized, starched and groomed as she was. All the while I was maneuvering so as to offer at all times a respectable front. A time or two Aunt Zo almost exposed my position, but I succeeded in breaking loose and bringing up the rear.

This being an exclusive neighborhood Papa had to take the team across town to a wagon yard. Parrying for time I made my play to go with him. En route I could present my problem and possibly kill two birds with one stone. One, Papa might consent to buy me another pair of pants. Two, he might not paddle me right there in public. But he vetoed my bid and it was during his absence that my true state was laid bare. I had wheeled to face the sudden arrival of a cousin, when Aunt Zo discovered my predicament. By quiet maneuvering she got me out and stitched me up without anyone else becoming the wiser. Unable to conceal my shame, or the source of it, I had played on the end of the thread like a bronc on a stake rope until she got me mended. All the while, bless her, she was trying to put me at my ease.

This "stitch in time" sent me skipping downstairs, ready to look the whole world in the face. Or better still, turn my back on it. The arrival of Jay, Mon, and Sog from the farm held no terrors for me now. I was the first to greet them at the door. However, to play it safe I called their attention to my haircut.

Suppertime found me so far removed from my recent state that I was beginning to show out. By bedtime I was impossible. And Papa, for some strange reason was allowing me more rope than usual, hoping, perhaps, that I would hang myself—which I was shortly to do.

"Bedtime, everybody."

An ultimatum too sad and too soon for me, until I learned that I would get to sleep with Jay and Sog. Put these two together and they were more comical than a medicine show and vaudeville combined. Put me between them and I'd have the equivalent of a box seat. Even if they put me at the foot of the bed—generally my lot—it would still be a bargain. Their feet were likewise funny.

With a *God's in his Heaven and all's right with the world* feeling I prepared for bed, in my case a procedure quicker done than said. Shuck shoes, pop out of pants and *presto* stripped to shirttail and ready to retire.

"My goshamighty, boy, what's that all over your ——?" yelled Jay, his voice sounding like he'd stepped on a rattler.

Stultified by sudden success, addled by excess attention, I had completely forgotten the cotton picker's itch!

"Why, it's nearly well now. You oughta seen it before," I said, hoping to mitigate the shock. But I could sense it without looking that the shock was not mitigated.

"What *is* that?"

"Aw, I ain't been well since Papa had me a-headin' that old maize," I said, my face redder than the affected areas.

"What's that he's got, Sog?"

"Itch, I expect. But he's supposed to of got shed of it," Sog said, sounding got off with. What's *he* got to be got off with I thought, sorrowfully. Think about me!

"Paul, come with me," Jay said, and started for the door. I couldn't determine by his expression where or what. I sort of hoped he wasn't leading me out to shoot me, and yet I halfway hoped he was. When he informed me I was to bathe, a shooting seemed preferable what with the grim, cold, draughty specter of a number-2 staring me in the face. But once confronted with a magnificent white bathtub of warm water in a steam-heated room I was again happy to stay alive. And such sweet scents—perfumes, lathers, lotions, and clean linens. Shortly, however, the sweet scents gave way to a sour, sulphurous smell.

"Soak awhile, Paul. And when you get through rub yourself all over good with this stuff," Jay said, motioning to a lotion on a little shelf nearby.

"Why, that's sulphur and grease!" I said, aghast, "What on earth could *you all* be doin' with a itch remedy?"

"Holler if you need anything," Jay said, and left, seeming to have misunderstood my remark.

Bathed and back in the bedroom I found a pallet in the far corner. I could take a hint. Thoughtful of him, though, to let me stay in the house. Besides, this beat having his feet in my face.

CHAPTER XXXVI

Maybe the *thirty-third* time was the charm, after all, for my career here at Balmorhea was beginning to parallel that of a new-rich, oil-rich Indian Ralph had run across in his ramblings; I was making more money than I knew what to do with.

"I know one thing. I'm not gonna take no three baths a day, put on new drawers and burn the others each time," I said, then could have bitten my tongue off for so doing. Left me wide open for more ridicule. Shades of the early Loraine days. And nights. Of late I had developed a new phobia, in this case *hydrophobia*, an unreasonable fear of water, which, I suppose, had been latent all along. This fear I could attribute to a trick they had pulled on me at Toyah Creek. Since the stream was only ten, maybe twelve, feet wide, they had wheedled and needled me into swimming it. When I was about midway out they began to yell *"sink hole! SINK HOLE!"*, a sink hole being to me now what nesters' rafters had been four years ago. Terrified beyond description I commenced splashing water for dear life. After I had crawled gasping and exhausted up yonder bank the following dialog took place:

"After we hollered sink hole, you see how well Paul swum that creek?" Ralph asked.

"Swum it? Why, he jist fought the water out of the way and walked out," Sog said.

"Papa says Paul's afraid of water. I say he's not," he went on. Then as a very loud aside: "Unless it is in, say, a number-2 tub."

Back to the present, as regards my remark: Ralph was saying, "Three baths a day? Of course you wouldn't." His remarks were perfectly innocent as to wordage but steeped in innuendo, calculated to humiliate and infuriate.

"If Paul does bathe he won't have to burn his clothes," Sog put in, "they'll catch fire by what you call spontaneous combustion."

"Nor will you ever catch Paul in silk drawers." This from Fush. "He's got to get used to cotton ones first."

Now, the trio, after Ralph had given the pitch:

> Paul got up old enough to shave
> And says "doggone it, Papa, I ain't big enough to bathe."

Then:

> Paul got up overcome with wrath
> And says "I dreamed Papa made me take a bath."

And:

> Paul got up a-streakin' for the brush . . . .

Quite by accident, here, I succeeded in stopping them cold, square in midverse with a perfectly innocuous remark, albeit uttered at the top of my lungs: "Me and that rich Indian. I'd give ever' cent I've made just to be poor again. If it'd make you all leave me alone."

Incredibly, this silenced them henceforth and forever—except for a brief flurry some three weeks later. We had returned from the hay fields one afternoon sodden and soggy from a sudden shower. Like saddle ponies after a downpour, everybody—except myself—was frisking and carrying on. All of a sudden Ralph grabbed me and stretched me flat on the porch.

"Come here, Sog," he called, beckoning with his chin since it took both hands and feet to keep me under control. "Looky here! Why, these *are* freckles. You told me they was spots from a bucket of molasses he kicked over back in Upland one time. If it hadn't been for this rain . . . "

"Shut up. Turn me a-loose."

"See that old buzzard yonder? A-settin' on that hackberry?" Sog was saying. "With wings spread that-a-way? Makes out like he's dryin' 'em. Actually, he's stayin' ready to fly off in case Paul gets too close." Here Ralph cut in:

"Yeah. The same one that was here last Sunday when Paul was asleep on the porch. Ain't he? The one that lit by him, puked, and flew off?"

"Yeah, that's him."

"Then, Paul, you better watch him, now that you're cleaner." And so on.

Whether this final infuriating incident rendered me impervious to the slings and arrows of my outrageous brothers or whether this summer shower lessened my fear of water in a number-2 tub I'll never know. But it left me with only the ordeal of a twelve-hour day, punching wires on a hay baler, and the worry of what to do with an ever-increasing hoard of silver. Each Saturday afternoon I walked the two miles into town and cashed my check at the bank, indifferent to the strain it must have put on that organization.

"Silver or bills?" the man in the black sleeves would ask.

"Silver."

Smiling, he would clink down nine silver dollars. The man was so friendly I was tempted to ask him the procedure one followed in depositing money. But this would make me appear too green. From the bank I would cut across to the Mercantile and stand in front a spell, mustering the courage to go inside and make my purchases. Timidity, not thrift, was the cause of my silver's corroding and cankering in a peach can out home. Strangely, the peach can meant more than the silver. It was the badge of affluence—symbolized more "fancies" among the "staples!"

Courage up I would sidle inside. With averted gaze and muffled voice I would stammer my order:

"Package of wax and ten cents of candy."

"This kind?"

"Yes'm."

With my sight unseen purchase I would duck out and head for the farm, despising myself—and my wealth. A hoard of silver beyond my wildest dreams and can't think of more than a fifteen-cent purchase. And if I could think of it I wouldn't have the guts to call for it. On the other hand, there was nothing else I wanted, really, except a saddle and a pair of shop-made boots. But whoever heard of saddle and boots without a horse and a cowboy job? Well, I did crave a bicycle but this too was out of the realm of reality. Papa had long since denounced bicycles as needless luxuries—living beyond one's means.

Though the root of many evils, this excess wealth had its compensations. For example, I could hire Fush occasionally, to do an onerous chore, for which he got well paid, and then some. He demanded—and received—more for slopping the hogs one time than the Pattersons *in toto* got for an all day's grubbing back in Roscoe. However, my money proved no good as a bribe—getting Gwen to tell Papa *she* had violated some domestic ordinance or another. Never did work out. She was too much like Papa—too incorruptibly honest, exasperatingly unbribable. Besides, it was worth more than mere money to her to tell Papa, "Paul done it."

CHAPTER XXXVII

By summer's end our combined savings must have hit an astronomical figure, for the big boys came home one evening with a bolt-out-of-the-blue announcement:

"We've bought us a automobile!"

"What kind?" I asked, visions of Cole 8s dancing in my head.

"Tin Henry."

"Where's it at?" This from the practical Fush.

"In town. Gettin' a overhaul."

"How old is it?" Fush again, his suspicions aroused by the word "overhaul."

"Smoothe mouth," Sog said. "Smoothe mouth" was a horse trader's term for "old enough" as well as a horse buyer's term for "too old."

"When will it get here?" I asked, half on the prod at Ralph for not bringing it on and overhauling it himself—in my presence. He had, for years, been solely responsible for the maintenance and upkeep of Granddad Pollard's Maxwell. But for the fact that Ralph still seemed like an uncle I'd have told him off. Again the question:

"When will it get here?"

"Day or two."

That day or two "crept in its petty pace from day to day to the last syllable of recorded time." Meantime, my waking hours were being assailed by anxieties and apprehensions, beset and besieged by nagging questions: How much of Papa's horse trading helplessness had been inherited? Or, can horse trading helplessness carry over into the machine age? That is to say, could my brothers have been as helpless in the hands of a used-car dealer as Papa has always been at the hands of horse traders?

"If this be-ust the case, Lord, helpest Thou us all!" I prayed, reverting to what I considered God's own dialect, for emphasis. "The prayers of a righteous man availeth much." Either I wasn't sufficiently righteous or was of little faith, for my apprehensions, anxieties, and doubts continued to assail, beset, and besiege. Already my mind's eye—and ear—had picked up the approach of our automobile—a rickety rattletrap, the machine age equivalent of old Heave Ho—spluttering, coughing, and wheezing and finally falling dead at our feet never to rise again.

Eventually, however, a brighter day dawned and Sog came herding it in, with Ralph as instructor and copilot. Fush and I, sighting the dust signal, had met it half a mile from the house and followed it at full cry.

"Whoa, Sog. Wait for us."

But it was a full quarter of a mile before Sog, new to the complicated manipulations of horseless carriages, could set the thing back on its haunches in a complete stop.

"Better let me take 'er on in, Sog," Ralph advised, "else we overshoot our destination.

Brief and bumpy notwithstanding, this paled all previous automobile rides into insignificance, Reed Buick excursions not excepted. Just something special about riding in one's own automobile. When Ralph brought the thing to a standstill, he and Sog jumped clear. But Fush and I stayed aboard for a tour of inspection, waiting for the dust to settle. Up until now we had been too wrapped up in the ride to take stock.

Dispelled with the dust cloud were my vision of Cole 8s. Dispelled also were some of the doubts, apprehensions, and anxieties.

Though not exactly a Cole 8, neither was it the automobile equivalent of a Heave Ho. That is to say, it's motor appeared to be in the finest fettle. However, when you've said that you've said it all —motor being about all there was to it except for a chassis and a battered cushion wired thereto. Even so it was a car! Our car! And a seven passenger one to boot—even if the last five aboard found it a pretty precarious perch!

As soon as visibility would permit we swarmed the auto, throwing levers, turning taps, tapping bolts, reading readings, pumping pedals, fighting over who would sit under the steering wheel, and so on. Presently we prevailed upon Ralph to crank her up so we could listen to her purr. Just as the magneta ignited the motor I was attracted by one of the pretty spark plugs. The reading thereon said "Champion" something. Champion Dempsey, I concluded, after what hit me. Naturally, I suspected Fush's skullduggery and was fixing to take appropriate measures when Ralph informed me it was electricity. Then he had to go into minute detail explaining how this wasn't an electric car but a gasoline one.

Despite frequent blowouts, breakdowns, stallings, and stampedes we Pattersons were making the transition into the machine age gratefully if not always gracefully. Even Papa, previously an adamant advocate of horsepower staying in the horse, succumbed. He began to demand his turns under the wheel. As a wagon chauffeur Papa knew no peers—a cool customer as the Roscoe runaway will attest—but under a steering wheel he was panic prone. Riding with him tended to temper my judgment of the hit-and-run autoist who snuffed out the life of old Philip. Papa was apt as not, unintentionally, of course, to run over his own children, much less a stray dog. With him at the wheel we weathered at least a runaway a day for at least thirty days.

Strangely enough, I was never panicky, in fact, never suffered even the faintest foreboding. Perhaps it was because there were no horizontal horse tails slapping me in the face, or no iron tires screeching like sirens at a four-alarm fire. Papa was invariably performing, out of sequence, the simple steps of driving—pumping the wrong pedal, lowering the wrong lever. His primary problem, however, was the accidental knocking down of the gas lever and then not knowing what he had done or what to do. Once this happened just as a big wooden gate loomed directly in our path. "What's good for the goose is good for the gander," he reasoned, so he cut sharply aside and started circling 'er like a runaway team. We laid down half a mile of mesquite before Ralph could take over. But for doing irreparable damage to Papa's pride, Ralph would have taken over much sooner in these frequent and sudden emergencies.

"She cold-jawed on me," Papa would always alibi, placing the blame entirely on the machine and thus salvaging a vestige of his pride. Though he wouldn't own up to it for the world he came to dread that T-model like a greenhorn cowboy dreads an outlaw horse, perhaps because of auto "horror stories" bruited about by early automobile owners. He, himself, admitted to having seen more gates laid down, more trees uprooted, and more walls caved in, and more stock killed by autos than he'd ever seen in the days of horse runaways and cow stampedes. What's more, kicking Tin Lizzies had accounted for more broken arms than kicking mules ever had.

"The self-starter," Papa was later to surmise, "is from a humane standpoint, a greater contribution than the electric chair." Then he went on to point out that although the self-starter took the kick out of the T's front end she was still snaky from the horse-accustomed old-timer's point of view. She could still cold-jaw, balk, run over or rear up and fall backwards on a man. Painful as Papa's transition to the machine age was, he eventually made it—almost. That is he learned to drive but never would trust the critter above 15 mph.

CHAPTER XXXVIII

One afternoon in early September the big boys were waiting at the schoolhouse when books let out for the day. I was thrice overjoyed: one, our automobile would improve our image with teachers and students alike, two, it meant another thrilling automo*bile* ride, three, it would save us a two-mile walk. Fush, however, seemed solemn, sorrowful. And for good reason—he smelled a mouse.

"Don't tell me; I'll tell you. Here comes *thirty-four*."

"Right. Hop on and we'll tell it on the road."

Papa had just chunked up his job and the big boys, prompted by that fierce independence that had prompted Papa, walked off with him. So what if Patterson purchasing power was greater than ever before? Freedom to go would take precedence over freedom to purchase any day. Besides, money in too large amounts had a tendency to curtail a man's freedom, to hobble him. Or at least put him on picket.

"Well," Papa had said to the boss, "since my work don't seem satisfactory I'm askin' for my time." Simple, on the surface and seemingly an irrational act on Papa's part. But such was not the case. He had been a section boss in charge of a certain area of alfalfa. Under his supervision were some eight or ten teamsters including Ralph, Sog, seven or eight Mexican-Americans, and a company executive's son.

It was Papa's responsibility to see that his crew made their daily quota of so many acres mowed and raked. Well, this big shot's son, reckless and smart-alecky to begin with, let his team run away this morning, hamstringing one of the horses and consuming the shank of the day patching up the damage. Result, Papa's crew had fallen far below its quota for the day. The way Papa looked at it it was the kid's place to speak up. But nary a peep out of him, hence *thirty-four* forthcoming. And where would it be this time? Fort Stockton, which sounded fair enough. It was sixty miles closer to Upland and, purportedly, a cow town. Best of all, there was the trip, and this time I stood a chance of making some of it in an automobile. But "the best laid plans of mice and men." I was left, along with Papa, Gwen, and Fush, to snail it along in the old Rock Island while Blanche, the big boys, and baggage were the ones to travel in style.

Such a turn of events cast a pall of gloom over the trip. In fact, it tended to cloud the future as well. The plodding, petty pace of the schooner was conducive to prolonged ponderings—ponderings of the past and prognostications of the future. Although we had been there six months—far beyond our average tenure—I now realized that Balmorhea had gotten a hold on me. I had learned to love its ring of shining mountains, its fast-running irrigation canals, and its friendly, freehearted kids. True enough it was farm-encircled, but just beyond these farms lay the mountains and in these mountains lay ranches, within which confines lay my dreams and aspirations. The day would have come when I grew up and would be there ridin', rippin', ropin', and runnin'. Although I didn't know how the action-prone Fush would have fared until that day, it would have occasioned no obstacles to an old pro daydreamer like myself. Here I found myself depressed enough to seek solace in the scriptures, and subliminally, I suppose, I hit upon "forgetting those things which are behind, and reaching forth unto those things which are before."

What was before *was* cow country and *was* sixty miles closer to Upland. What's more our automobile would enhance our acceptance by the Stocktonites (and Fush could take care of those who didn't). On top of that I would—provided I could locate the peach can—flash as much cash money as any kid in school. All of a sudden I found myself whistling "Casey Jones," and as further evidence of a lift in spirit, I quit the schooner on the run to join Fush in his scouting excursions.

CHAPTER XXXIX

From the heights back into the depths. Twenty-four hours into *thirty-four* and my heart was yearning for *thirty-five*. We had landed square in the middle of clodhopper country again, doing the very same drudgery we had done in Balmorhea, but without the beautiful, pleasant surroundings. What's more our automobile and better clothes would by no means ensure our immediate and complete acceptance by the Stockton small fry. We were going to have to prove ourselves in other—and possibly violent—ways.

Aside from our first day at school the four-month stretch in this irrigated cotton and alfalfa community was routine misery and dull, monotonous pain. But better routine misery and dull, monotonous pain than that excruciating first day, a day ranking with the wild mule chase, the sailor straws, the JM ghost, and other near-catastrophes I had experienced with the peril-prone Fush.

This most miserable of days began with the catching of the school bus. Once aboard I realized we were among the strangest of strangers—kids speaking English with an accent that was not Spanish, the only two languages I thought were in existence. If their language was strange their behavior was doubly so. We hadn't gone a hundred yards until a gigantic, foreign girl fetched me a clout up side the head that made my ears ring for the next two days. Fush's rigid cowboy code of never striking a woman, I figured, was all that saved his life. This girl had done this to me in high good humor. Angered, what would she have done to Fush?

When we reached the school grounds, by some tragic circumstance I got cut off from Fush, but before I could rush off in search of him I found myself completely encircled by boys. Still sharply mindful of what a specie of Stockton's weaker sex had done to me my mainmost thought here, framed into a silent prayer was: "Have thine own way, Lord. Not their'n."

Being cut off from Fush by a mob like this, to my way of thinking, was like being kicked out of a wagon train in Sioux country twenty-four hours after Custer's last stand. Two tiers of terror assailed me. First, I feared for my hide. Second, without Fush's example, I would crack, show the white feather, under the gauntlet these savages would put me through. Two of the leaders were already maneuvering for position.

"Mornin', fellers," I croaked, my exterior calm, but my interior completely in the hands of pandemonium. The ringleader, with somewhat horizontal upper teeth, jerked my hat down over my eyes then shoved me backward over his crouching henchman. This opening act drew a laugh from the crowd and, consequently, inspired the actors to greater efforts. While I was picking myself up Buckteeth turned to the crowd and in a melodramatic tone announced:

"And now, ladies and gentlemens, I'll nowby perceed to take his britches off."

Ladies? My heart sank even lower as my eye verified this fact. The cold but expectant faces—even of the two or three "ladies" present—foretold of no help forthcoming. Nor would there be pity, except that emanating from me. Here the Teeth closed in. Vowing to sell myself dearly, to uphold the Patterson honor—and trousers—I put up a terrific tussle, which fact surprised me as much as it did him. Since Fush had always done my physical contact work I didn't really know my own strength in a pinch.

"Gosh, I don't believe Elmo's gonna git that new boy down."

This sideline observation was ammonia to my suffocating spirit. I threw my last ounce of strength into the struggle but to no avail. Shortly, Elmo was sitting a-straddle my stomach.

"Unbuckle his belt, Frank," he said to his partner in crime, "and unbutton his britches."

"You low-down scoun'els," I screamed, bucking and kicking like old Heave Ho. But Elmo and Frank, apparently, were old hands at this game. Elmo kept his seat and Frank kept making progress with my pants.

"I druther you beat me half to death than . . . "

My remark was clipped in mid-sentence by a loud *thonk*. Abruptly the tugging at my pants ceased. Another, louder *thonk* and Elmo toppled to one side.

"These dirty sons o' b——guns hurt you, Paul?"

Over me stood Fush, wild-haired, wild-eyed and with a wagon spoke in his hand.

"No, but they was a-takin' my britches off," I said, on the verge of bawling, even if I was in Fush's presence and ten years old. But now I had a special incentive for holding off. Elmo and Frank, both on their feet again, were bawling a discordant duet. By holding off I could prove *I* was a better man.

"Bow-w-w-w-w-w-," said Elmo, caressing a growing lump on his head, "you don't fight fair."

Fush handed me the wagon spoke and turned to face him.

"Looky here, Punkin Eater, I s'pose it's fair—you two pickin' on this pore little child." In cases of this kind Fush referred to me as "this pore little child." But I supposed he was justified, being a full year and a half older.

"It's fair now. Let's go after it."

"My head hurts too bad. But I'll—I'll . . . "

"How about you, then?" Fush challenged, turning to Frank.

"I'll get even with you. I will." said Frank, but without conviction.

"Right now's your chance. While you got me hemmed up."

But Frank, like Elmo, was through for the day. And then some.

The mob, however, was still hostile at the way Fush had taken care of their leaders. Mob psychology at work, they tightened the circle around us, all the while muttering threats. But not very loudly what with that wagon spoke back in capable and willing hands.

When Fush took the weapon from me I realized we were at bay. That is, Fush was at bay; I was treed. Since being treed, I understand, means that one has no fight left.

"Ever who ain't satisfied step up. I'll fight you fair and square, but I'm pertectin' this child with *this*." No great utterance, grammatically or otherwise, but plain enough for the mob. Nobody was satisfied, of course, but nobody was dissatisfied enough to hear that wagon spoke speak again.

"All right then," Fush warned, "stand to one side. We're a-comin' out."

The crowd opened as we strode, like Napoleon and orderly, through the ranks. Fush had taken their measure for certain. I was positive this bunch would never lay finger on me again. That is unless they caught me—highly improbable—away from Fush.

Thus ended our trouble with a pugnacious portion of the Stockton student body. But we arrived at the schoolhouse to learn that the Stockton principal had taken up the fight. We were to report to his office after school.

"What you reckon he'll do, Fush?"

"At least he won't take yore britches off—just down a ways."

"Don't tease me, Fushhhhhh," I whimpered, the old forebodings back at the forefront.

"You didn't do anything. He won't whip you. I'll fix things up with him. Honest."

Fush's ability to perform miracles notwithstanding, I couldn't allay that ever-at-hand anxiety.

With the tolling of the four o'clock *knell*, I sought out Fush and together we sought out the principal. He was a broad, blocky man who put me in mind of the outlaw Poggin in Zane Grey's *Lone Star Ranger*. Two slugs from a .45 couldn't have drilled through us any quicker or straighter than those steely eyes. He motioned us to a bench upon which sat, or rather, squirmed, Elmo and Frank.

His cross examination was brief, brusque. Trial concluded he paddled Elmo and Frank for assault and battery (and attempted indecent exposure—of me), Fush for simple assault, and acquitted me. Then after having us shake hands all around he dismissed the other two and turned those .45 slug eyes on Fush.

"William!"

"Yes, sir. Sir?" said Fush, but only after I'd informed him whom the man meant.

"William, *never* ever let me hear of you striking those two with a wagon spoke again. Hear?"

"Yes, SIR. I mean NO, SIR. I mean . . . "

"Make it something more substantial. Say, like a pee ellum club. You are dismissed," he said, the awesome solemnity of his expression suddenly dissipated by a wide grin.

CHAPTER XL

Our social status secured, I was no longer ashamed to look any grown Stocktonite in the eye; just as I was no longer afraid—with Fush's backing—to meet the eye of the little ones. School relations and conditions had improved to the extent that we no longer hid under the culvert and told Blanche we missed the bus. Our last real unpleasant incident was now quite a few days in the past. This was when Madge (with us now, since Grandma Pollard's death) had had to slap a big girl's jaws for making fun of Gwen's coat. Which act made her more of a sister than an aunt even though only an aunt, we figured, would have taken on a girl that big and that old.

Improved relations notwithstanding, it was with great rejoicing we received the news of upcoming *thirty-five*.

"Where to, Papa?"

"Rankin."

"RANKIN?"

"*Rankin?*"

"R-A-N-K-I-N, *Texas?*"

"Rankin, Texas!"

From Blanche on down with each succeeding question growing more incredulous in tone, for Rankin was practically next door to our old Upland paradise.

176

After a sudden soaring of spirits, the likes of which hadn't been seen since our old Upland days, from the heights to the depths again in my case. Only in the poems of Edgar Allen Poe would one find lines that could accurately depict the depths of my despond.

And my soul from out that shadow that lies floating on the floor
Shall be lifted nevermore.

Just as in *eight* through *thirty-four* respectively, I had been assigned (condemned) to the covered wagon for *thirty-five*. The automobile was reserved exclusively for the exclusives—Ralph, Sog, Blanche, and Madge. Some consolation in the fact, however, that they would be camping with us at night, thus demonstrating to passersby that this wasn't a bunch of rawhiders—a straight-out horse-drawn outfit.

One modern means of transportation notwithstanding this trip was on the rawhiders' order. Once Fush and I became resigned to frontier-type travel we decided to adapt to frontier means of subsistence—living off the land. Besides, our fare was back down to straight staples—the barest of staples at that. So, to complement the sowbelly and sorghum Fush shot a curlew bird which we attempted to cook and eat, with both attempts ending in total failure. It took Ralph and his poetry to put the situation in its proper perspective:

Look, a curlew never try to cook.
But if you ever do
A curlew you will never, never, never chew.

Although it didn't take a curlew to tell us our food left much to be desired, we felt that our shelter was adequate. That is, until all of a sudden, a blue blizzard—with a graying, alkali tinge—whistled down upon us. The biting, piercing wind forced us to pool our pallets under a common, or community, covering. We waived Papa's iron-clad tradition of always bedding down with heads to the north—to allow the earth's natural currents to flow from head to foot, and taking the 8' x 16' tarp from Sog's cowboy roll and

lapping it, horizontally, under and over the upwind end, we succeeded in blunting to some extent the cruel edge of the elements.
Even so it still didn't set well with a cold curlew and canned-corn
supper. (After Balmorhea, we no longer considered canned corn
"fancy".) Nor could it compensate for a campfire that couldn't
quite cut the accumulated chill of the day. Consequently, gloom
as well as chill had settled over camp.

"Thick as seven in a bed." Pause. "In fact thicker—they's eight
of us." Sog hollered above the howl of the norther. It took Sog to
break the ice, to take the chill out of an otherwise cold world. This
warmed us to other well-timed witticisms of his back down the
moving years. For example, the earth-bottomed shack Ralph had
rented for them in Breckenridge.

"How you like it, Sog?"

"Why wouldn't I like it? You've got us in on the ground floor."

Before conversation died that night many were the pranks and
wisecracks recalled whereby Sog had brightened our road and
lightened our load. Blanche had summed it up like this: "Bound for
Sog to show us that there is a bright, light side to every thing every-
where."

Still smarting from the schooner and suffering from a seizure of
self-pity I couldn't help but strike a negative note:

"Yes, but what about that time he read me that 'Road to Hell'
sign on the gate?" The answer came from Sog himself.

"Bright side to that too, Paul. Shore feels like we're headed in
the opposite direction tonight."

Because of extreme cold and scarcity of water—plus our aversion to it—Fush's and my hands rusted and cracked open. From this
ailment I suffered audibly most of my waking hours, little dreaming that these rasp-like fists were shortly to stand me in good stead.
The night after we landed in Rankin, Tom Schnaubert hemmed
me in and forced me to fight my way out. With a flurry of raspy
fists I blazed a trail to safety. The poor kid thought I was hitting
him in the face with a mad porcupine.

CHAPTER XLI

The tail end—always the ridiculous one—of our caravan rolled into Rankin the day school let out for Christmas, 1920. Our old friends the Garners, the Lanes, the Collinses, plus a few hospitable strangers were on hand to extend to us the key to the city. Happy as Fush and I were to see them we would have preferred they wait until we had gotten clear of the covered wagon. Automobile notwithstanding, we found ourselves as self-conscious of the schooner as we had been of the sailor straws. But typical of Rankin citizenry they received us with open arms. Rankin was not only a hospitable city but a paradise on earth—not a stalk of cotton, a head of maize, or a stem of alfalfa growing within fifty miles. This was ranch country. And consequently, God's. I shuddered at the prospect of *thirty-six*—unless it was locally.

Even though we owned an automobile, we landed in Rankin with little more cash reserves than the seventy-five cents that carried us through the first few days at Upland. Again, as Papa put it, "we were startin' from the stump." As if the evils of this day were not sufficient thereof the girls' valise had bounced off the auto and was lost for good. Papa, still not one to live beyond his means, rented the only house in town he could afford to pay a month's rent in advance—$1.50.

"Not quite on the ground floor," as Sog put it, "but at rock bottom."

Papa, with no working or waiting capital, cast about desperately for a job, and characteristic of Patterson luck, landed a contract.

"Doggone it," Ralph said, more in jest than in earnest, "Papa would make out all right if we could just keep him from comin' in contact with strangers with runny-nosed kids."

Papa's contract was with the telephone company, taking down the phone line from Upland to Rankin (our last connection and communication with our first paradise). Not finding Rankin the paradise we did, Ralph lit a shuck for greener pastures. Sog immediately signed on "study" with the Booger Y and went back to the *only* profession, something Fush and I dreamed of doing the minute Papa would hold still for it. This, unfortunately, would not be in the foreseeable future. Papa still brooded, and sometimes openly, over our missing that year of schooling at Roscoe and Loraine. Now he seemed as set in his ways about our being educated as he was in his choice of boys' hats and man's jobs. He was humiliatingly old-fashioned about these things but disgustingly modern as regards education.

Typical of Papa and his contracts it was touch and go the rest of the winter over who would act as official doorman, Papa or the wolf. But typical and characteristic of Papa at no time—then, before, or since—was one Patterson "on the county" one minute. And this is more than can be said of at least two families whose breadwinner was a better trader and contractor than Papa.

Sadly, Fush and I enrolled in Rankin Grammar School. Shortly, however, we were overjoyed to learn that only a small part of Rankin life was books. It had its extracurricular activities—the penning and riding of milk pen calves, stray yearlings, loose burros, loose buggies coasting downhill, loose chickens to paint red or to eat, box cars to jump off of, and many more diversions more or less legal. Many of these practices, frowned upon by the adult population, had to be carried on under cover of darkness. Thus our book learning went on by day and our cowboy training by night.

For the first night or two I applied myself diligently to night school but soon grew discouraged. The course proved too rugged. I had forgotten that an apprenticed cowboy had to have so much nerve. I wondered if there weren't cowboy correspondence courses for my type. Fush, of course, soon achieved high marks in night school along with other great potential cowboys such as the Collins boys, Alton Holland, Jap and Clay Taylor, Lee Lane, June Garner, and Bud Monroe. In fact, every kid in town, except myself and Fatty Sammons, was making remarkable progress. Not that Fatty was lacking in skill and courage; there wasn't a beast in town big enough to test his horsemanship.

Any one of them could ride the roughest bull yearling in the bunch. Hopelessly surrounded I could be hoodwinked onto this black bull but he invariably strung me up in the nearest mesquite, crammed me under a fence, or jammed my head in fresh cow tracks. All this in spite of their constant tutoring. Even so, my cowboy aspirations remained unwavering. But hereafter I would seek my goal more through correspondence than through residence work.

Contributing factors toward my unswerving cowboy aspirations were the volumes of western fiction I consumed via *Wild West Weekly*, *Western Story*, *Ace High*, and the real west that was closer than hands and feet. True, it was less subject to violence— except when they forcibly slung me astride old Midnight—but it was no less colorful, especially during the fall of the year. For days the stock pens would spill over and the town would vibrate with the bawl of cattle and the jingle of spurs. Fires of half a dozen chuck wagons batted and blinked from all sides as different outfits held herds on hills and draws, waiting room to pen and ship out. Even the strong, musky smell of hide, horn, and hoof borne upon stifling streamers of dust, was entrancing to a cowboy-prone kid.

One night a freight train boogered a herd of twelve hundred big 7f steers. Laying down the entire north side of the stock pens they scattered to hell and gone. What joy! No matter to me if it did take the outfit thirty days to regather. Just like the old "Thirty-One Years on the Plains and in the Mountains" days.

To keep alive such stirring incidents I would envision myself as a leading part of it. Plunging headlong down the stock pens hill I would shake out a quick loop, dab it on the rocking horns of an outlaw steer and catch the admiring yells of the lesser cowboys as they skylighted the critter coming down broadside. An alternate daydream was one in which I pictured myself coming off that same hill playing a Kelly brothers duet high in the shoulders of a wicked-pitching black bronc. As the grand finale I would see myself around camp that night attacked by a bully with the chuck wagon's breast yoke. Yanking it from his grasp, I would toss it aside and beat the bully's ears down—right there in front of Mabel Lane, Lelezelle Monroe, Mayanna Yates, and everybody.

All of these dreams in progress, of course, while Fush and the other boys were actually plunging headlong down the stock pens hill in a Fush-and-Jap-Taylor guided buggy, catching freight trains out to the grade, jumping off boxcars onto the depot, all of which perilous pursuits weren't worth the wear and tear on my nervous system. But I was always with them when swimming season came upon us. Our swimming hole—in season, meaning anytime there was rain or hail—was a washout in the big draw that ran westward through the outskirts of town. If it rained or hailed or even snowed, we bathed regularly. If it didn't, we didn't.

Although the *lake* was a scant two hundred yards from downtown Rankin, a thick growth of catclaw and mesquite afforded us absolute privacy. However, the old swimming hole tradition of "last one in's a rotten egg" worked at cross purposes with these sheltering bushes. Every kid in town—including myself eventually—would be stripped stark naked before the fastest of us reached the brush. Wild West dreamer and reader that I was, I never missed a daily bath or two as long as there remained a foot of water therein. Many's the time we've submerged and emerged through an inch coat of hailstones whereas, a number-2 tub of lukewarm water would have set our teeth to chattering and brought on our "death of cold."

CHAPTER XLII

My life heretofore had been spent in comparative isolation, rural surroundings exclusively, with the exception of Upland (which was really no exception since the General Mercantile had left before we moved to town). Now, this strange, new "city life" environment had wrought a change in me, and not for the better. Little for my age and dumb for my size notwithstanding, I had quickly picked up a knack for squandering, and shortly this knack had developed into a fine art, even though "squanderlust" in the Patterson household would seem as likely of fulfillment as wanderlust in the Count of Monte Cristo.

Long gone was the contempt I once held for the filthy lucre (having connected it with the type who had run down old Philip). Likewise long gone was the easy money—$1.50 for a 12–14 hour day—in the Balmorhea hayfields, for which I now harbored a burning yen. Money, that is. (A brief interpolation here to say that Blanche had banked my Balmorhea savings to the amount of $51.50 and taught me how to write checks, thus inadvertently committing two grave errors.) Now this burning yen for money had put me within a short arm's length of the long arm of the law.

This latent lawlessness in me was brought to sudden fruition by *Western Story* magazine, but not in the manner one would assume. Not by constant exposure to gunsmoke and gore but by casual exposure to an advertisement. I was flipping feverishly the pages to pick up the tail end of the third installment of Robert Ormond Case's gripping "Yukon Trail" when my eye fell upon—or was speared by—a pointing finger backed up by a pair of hypnotic eyes. Do you want to earn quick, easy money in your spare time? Absolutely. Back when money was neither quick nor easy, I had earned it. And Lord knows I had spare time—spare, and heavy, until next week's installment of "Yukon Trail" what with Slim's and Rondo's and Lawson's herd scattered to hell and gone above Whitehorse and Rondo's girl mad at him to boot.

This forceful fellow (whose pointing finger may as well have been the barrel of a forty-five, such was the power it now held over me) went on to say he would send me a dozen boxes of Rosebud Salve. This marvelous household remedy I was to sell like hotcakes to a grateful public, pocket a generous commission, and mail the paltry remainder back to the salve people at my own convenience. Ordinarily one to procrastinate I immediately signed on the dotted line and raced this ad to the post office.

Interminable ages later in came this marvelous household remedy ready to be snapped up, hot-cake-like, by a poison-ivy smitten, insect-bitten, barber's itchy, chapped, muscle strained, chilblained, piles-pained (plus innumerable embarrassing ailments-ridden) public. Snatching up this salve-ation of mankind I sped out to make that quick, easy money. But the instant my feet hit the threshold of the first would-be customer, feet (and enthusiasm) turned ice cold.

What if Mrs. Sammons didn't suffer from chilblains, blind, bleeding, and protruding piles, or other embarrassing ailments like the label accused? Yet wouldn't my very presence insinuate as much? Not only to her but to her neighbors? Casting a quick, furtive glance in the direction of the door, I whirled on silent feet and slunk home, suddenly fearful of being indicted for some sort of slander. Here I held the remedy for all the ills that human flesh is heir to—relief for all the suffering citizens in Rankin. But I would let them suffer.

As quietly as I had sneaked off the first prospect's porch I let the matter drop, realizing that forty acres of alfalfa or even twenty-three of maize didn't look as forbidding as a citizen confronted with the assumption that he was a victim of blind, bleeding, and protruding piles. Nor was I letting a single soul into my confidence, especially Papa. He held certain hard-headed beliefs to the effect that one must finish a job come hell or high water.

Somehow I couldn't shake the uneasy hunch (as pronounced as Blanche's premonitions that always panned out) that the salve incident hadn't healed. My hunch was 100 per cent accurate. Directly a letter from the pointing man, the finger more than ever the semblance of a forty-five barrel. The letter, once opened, wasn't quite as formidable as the envelope would indicate. Though only a slight switch in substance from the ad there were sinister undertones between the lines:

Dear young salesman:
   Since our product has been a rapid seller we are at a loss to understand why our small share of the proceeds hasn't already reached our offices. Trusting that, if this remittance isn't already in the mails you will post it forthwith.

Very truly yours,
S. S. So-and-So, Sales Manager
Rosebud Salve Company

Though not as urgent as the original ad in which the pointing man pointed out the ease with which quick money could be made (and the leisure with which it could be remitted) the message left me visibly disturbed. Still I didn't take Papa into my confidence, nor even Fush who was devoting much of his time to riding lessons. Involving him might get me deeper involved in the riding lessons. I would let things *ride*; maybe time would tend to salve things over.

Two tense weeks snailed by and then letter number two. When

Blanche handed it over, I took it, wracked with the same emotion the old woman in the song must have experienced when they handed her that "letter edged in black." Only this one was to re-remind me that I was in the red. Retiring to the privacy of the privy I ripped it open and read:

Young Sir:
Some time ago we wrote you regarding the small sum of one dollar ($1.00) which was to have been enclosed as our share of profits accrueing from the sale of twelve (12) boxes of Rosebud Salve. Since the above-mentioned letter was not returned to us marked "unclaimed" we have reason to suspect that you are deliberately withholding our rightful share of the profits and that by so doing can call down upon yourself, and family, the full forces of the law. [A long sentence indeed, but not nearly so long as the one that came to mind. The letter concluded]: Unless this remittance is in our offices no later than June 4, 1921, we shall be forced to take legal steps.

Sincerely,
[A frightfully impressive though illegible signature and then]
S. S. So-&-So, President
Rosebud Salve Company

I didn't know exactly what "legal steps" meant but could infer by the tone of the letter that they were in some way connected to the steps of the jailer ringing on the iron floor twice daily as he came to shove my cornbread and molasses through the bars. (Shades of the prison house before the growing boy—only my growth, as of now, was arrested.) Bad enough should this come to pass in my beloved Upland, much less some cold, dark prison up north some place.

My first attempt at replacing the letter in the envelope was futile because of trembling hands. Likewise the second, for now my eye had fallen upon the *backing* on the envelope. This time the trembling hands were triggered not only by fear but by fury. *Master*

Paul Patterson! Master of what? Ninety-nine years, while I slaved over a rock pile somewhere? How cynical, how ironical can one get?

No time for forebodings, for broodings, for rankling resentments. What to do? Go directly to Papa or confide in Fush first? He was practical, and coolheaded for the most part. On the other hand he was subject to hotheaded spells albeit brief. No, not Fush in this case. His first impulse might be to use this very letter for the same purpose Sears catalog at my feet now served, which brash and brazen act would likely get us both shot on the spot. In the face of this mental picture, fear of Papa vanished, or at least diminished to the extent that I would make a clean breast of the whole shady business. Buckling my suspenders (to make the trip look legitimate) en route to the house I sought out Papa and unbosomed the whole sordid mess.

Papa, no orator by the widest stretch of the imagination, certainly extended himself that day. He unleashed upon me an oration of such clarity, eloquence, and force that I commenced, half-heartedly, to yearn for the old-fashioned strappings of yore. But he gave me the dollar, thus snatching me from those "shades of the prison house before the growing boy," and thereby stimulating the reassumption of growth. This dollar was not only salve to an uneasy mind and conscience but salve for the whole Patterson household for years to come.

CHAPTER XLIII

Although my first fling at free enterprise had resulted in the complete stifling of my enterprise, Papa was prospering after a fashion. We were now in a position to move to a *two*-story house a couple of hundred yards up the street. We called it the White House, not because of the few scattered scales of paint still clinging thereto but because it made us feel like the First Family. We wished for Mama because this would be the nearest thing to a home of her own since the five-room house in Midland. Move *thirty-six* might be the charm—if we could raise the exorbitant $4.00 per month rent.

Evacuating the shanty hard by the tracks was a lift to our ego and a compensation for my harrowing experience with the Rosebud people. Moving day found Papa off on a contract, so Sog was called in from the Y to supervise and superintend the job. His quick quips and compulsion for clowning, however, proved more detrimental than his strong hands were helpful. About time we'd have a heavy object hoisted halfway to the wagon bed he would strike us helpless with a witticism. *Kerblammm.* Down would go the three of us—Fush, I, and a piece of furniture, one of us to suffer irreparable damage. *Thirty-six*'s toll was a cracked cookstove, a leg amputated from a bureau, and a small dishpan of china busted to smithereens.

"That's what you'd call breakin' up housekeepin'," quipped the family philosopher.

Thus had move *thirty-six* of a mere two hundred yards proved more destructive than the two-hundred-mile trek from Roscoe to Balmorhea. Consequently, the expense would have been prohibitive had these items been retired from use. Fortunately the lame-legged condition of stove and bureau wouldn't directly affect me who neither cooked nor looked into mirrors. But the destruction caused no little anguish and humiliation among the girls, which anguish (with overtones of anger) they expressed in no uncertain terms. Sog was repentant, apologetic to the extreme, and Fush also to a lesser degree. But as for me, I was indifferent if not a bit insolent.

"Dern the looks; it still cooks," I cracked.

"Yes, but it's how it looks while it cooks," Blanche replied, not the least appreciative of the laughs I had strained at a camel and swallowed a gnat for. I started to parry her thrust but thought better of it. Even Sog with his deft delivery and perfect timing had judiciously left off levity. The master diplomat himself was walking softly, treading lightly. In fact it wasn't until he was mounted on a fast Y cow pony and outward bound that he reined in at the kitchen door and delivered his parting repartee:

"Blanche, you'll turn out to be a jim dandy cook one of these days if ..."

"If what?," she said, bristling.

"If a cookstove don't fall on you."

"Ohhhhhhhh," Blanche said, fighting back a grin.

"And Madge ..."

"I know. I'll turn out a right purty gal, if a bureau don't fall on me," she said, beating him to the draw. "And you'd have turned out a pretty good jackass, if a horse hadn't fallen on you." Life had laid a lighter hand on Madge, and its serious side was still some distance ahead.

Only after months and months of accumulating purchase coupons from B. S. Taylor & Company store were we able to replace the crippled cooker with a majestic new six-holer range with warming closet above, hot-water well in back, broiler on the side, and enough silver-nickeled ornamentation thereon to decorate every stove in town. But what caught our fancy was the white oven door, the material of which was forever after the subject of controversy. Fush said it was china, I said it was ivory, Madge said it was porcelain, Blanche said it was neither, but for some mysterious reason she would not reveal the exact substance. It turned out to be enamel, a material that emitted small flakes when struck overly hard, hence Blanche's mysterious silence. Many's the time she had apprehended me and Fush whacking pots and washpans with a stick and then putting an ear to them to enjoy the clicking sounds the shedding flakes gave off.

In commiseration to this splendid stove, *thirty-seven* was postponed for almost three years, the longest span ever. Meantime, Papa or Blanche kept constant vigil over the range and over us. And well they should have, for this cooker turned out to be the mesquite-eatingest, crosstie gobblingest critter we ever owned. As official woodcutter of the family frequent were my thoughts of doing it bodily harm, but by the time I got it stoked I was too weak for the task.

CHAPTER XLIV

Iron disciplinarian notwithstanding, the chief executive tolerated situations here at the White House that would have set Job to biting nails and rending mantles. First it was love; now it was war. Love had settled into a peaceful routine now that B had become Madge's ex. The Taylor boys, Grimm, then Lewis, courted quietly, politely and said their fond farewells at a reasonable hour. The same could be said of Herbert Holmes, Blanche's beau.

The course of true love now running smooth, Papa was free to concentrate his full forces against war—war in the guise of slumber parties Fush and I were throwing upstairs. Love, however, became the unwitting accomplice of war when Herbert married Blanche and thus spirited away Papa's strongest ally. Madge, too near our age and too inexperienced, couldn't keep the peace during Papa's absences. Where Papa once had to rush into the parlor to separate lovers he was now having to plunge upstairs to mediate between warring factions. Fatty Sammons, though no longer a menace to mankind, was still murder on household furnishings both stable and fancy. Fush, Jap, Clay, Lee Lane, Bill Collins, Alton Holland, and June Garner, though not as big, were just as bouncy. Now that we were using more humane weapons—pillows instead of cowchips— I was to be reckoned with also.

Only after Papa had plunged back into politics (around 1922) was he able to bring order out of chaos. Politics kept him closer home thus allowing him to keep a closer eye on love and war. Even though he may have lost the vote of a lover or two (and would have lost all warriors' had they been eligible) he was making a bid for the county judge's office, which move had triggered traumas in us kids. His unorthodox approach to the election, and electioneering, afforded Fush and me much concern over his political future. Whereas the old pros would take a week off to kiss babies and two hours for a speech, Papa would take a chew of tobacco. When election day drew nigh we urged him to prepare a campaign speech larded liberally with pledges, promises, projects, and predictions. But our urgings fell on deaf ears. If there was anything that left Papa cold it was too many words of any kind, much less big ones. The next time Sog rode in from the Y's, we put our problem to him.

"Don't worry about Papa," Sog assured us, "let him be his own self and he could win a political race kissin' babies with a chew of Tinsley in his mouth. And passin' out loaded cigars."

Still we were not to be reassured. Papa didn't have the education for a judge, or the mien and manner. Or the belly. His face was too sun-seared; his hands too big, knotty, and calloused. Worse yet he still clung to the horse-drawn age, and our household furnishings were more in keeping with a city scavenger's. But our fears proved groundless; Sog's prophecy was fulfilled. Papa swamped the opposition something like 109 to 19.

Maybe the electorate knew what it was voting about after all, for we were downright proud of Papa the first time we saw him preside over a session of county court—proud even though he was hard put to keep from dozing during the long harangues. We were proud, not because he reminded us of a judge now, but because he reminded us of the village blacksmith in the poem. The blacksmith's hands, the blacksmith's eyes—blue, steady, honest eyes that could "look the whole world in the face, for he owed not any man" (despite the constant and continuous pressure from us kids). Proud likewise of his suit of clothes, complete with necktie, which latter appeared to gall him worse than a tight throatlatch on a "heavey" mule.

CHAPTER XLV

Pressure, prestige of office, tempo of the times—something eventually compelled Papa to succumb to the machine age. He swapped Babe, Nell, and the old Rock Island (now topless) to Dr. McDonald for an ancient motor truck of doubtful ancestry. From the engine forward it was a T-Model Ford but from there back it was a solid-tired something dreamed up in the fertile mind of young Box McDonald, its creator. Unlike losing those other loved ones to Dutch, parting with Babe and Nell was "such sweet sorrow." Doctor McDonald, a kindly, gentle man, would give them a better home than they had ever known. Not only would he furnish them with all the corn and alfalfa they could eat on his Pecos River farm, but he would keep their teeth in shape to chew. What's more they would evermore be spared humiliation such as I had subjected them to only a week before.

An elderly widower had hired, or contracted, me to plow up a garden patch, which tedious and harrowing task took Babe, Nell, and myself the better part of a lengthening spring day.

"How much I owe ye?" inquired the old gentleman in a most genial manner. Not only genial but generous, I figured, since he was flourishing a long, gar-mouth purse that not only tinkled of silver but crinkled of folding money.

Like Father; Like Son! I heard myself saying: "As Papa says, 'let your conscience be your guide.' "

It turned out the old gentleman had no *guide*. Now that sagging upon the plow handles wasn't from weariness alone. A greater part of it was from shock. *He had handed me a dime!*

Finally, and frankly, the parting with Babe and Nell would mean that another motor vehicle would regain social status that we surely must have lost when the Balmorhea T-model collapsed last winter. Yes, it had expired under circumstances similar to, and as sudden as, the demise of Heave Ho. A couple of wheezing, choking sighs and that was it. Here I couldn't help but feel bitterness along with the deep sorrow—bitterness at Ralph for being out of pocket at the time; with his professional services available perhaps the seizure wouldn't have proven fatal.

Whether this brand new (to us) motor vehicle improved our social standing we were not given time to find out. Papa judged by day, freighted by night, and saw to it that Fush and I kept equally as busy. It was against his principles for us to refuse the offer of any job whatsoever, regardless of wage, age, hours, or condition of servitude. For a cow country, Rankin could turn up more un-cowboy tasks than Loraine, Roscoe, Balmorhea, and Stockton put together—stump-grubbing, weed-hoeing, ditch-digging, wood-cutting, coal-hauling, and an occasional sheep-herding job. But for my grubby, threadbare appearance I'd have gone the Rosebud route. Balmorhea hours were much longer, but, oh, so much easier. And the Loraine maize-itch would seem soothing compared to blistered, bleeding hands and an ever-aching back.

Money, as usual, came hard for Fush and me. And went easy. Money making—and keeping—is doubtless an inherited talent as is a gift for art or music. Other Rankin boys seemed to always have it jingling in their overalls. Even Fush managed to hold onto some of it some of the time. Not me. Wordsworth's "late and soon, getting and spending" fit me to a T. The saddest of spectacles, say the thrifty, is a spendthrift spending hard-earned money. But a sadder one is a spendthrift speeding to Taylor & Co. Mercantile only to discover that he has lost the hard-earned five-dollar bill he had received for five bitter days of sheepherding, as was my lot that summer.

Not that it was any consolation, under the circumstances, but I learned that poor contracting ability ran in other families as well as our own. Bud Monroe and I contracted to dig old Doc Cushman a storm cellar twelve by eight by seven for $10. When the old gentleman pointed out that this would only amount to twenty cubic yards, a piddling bit of dirt for such an exorbitant sum of 50 cents a yard. Ridiculous. Feeling like two coyotes caught in a chicken house we immediately dropped our bid to $8.00. What we hadn't taken into account was the fact that since this dirt hadn't been tampered with in, say, four, possibly six billion years it could be pretty set in its ways. Nor had we considered the possibility of striking limestone or caliche, despite the fact that every digger in Rankin had struck this substance twelve to fourteen inches beneath the surface.

The two-dollar discount notwithstanding, we lit into the soft bosom of Mother Earth still proud of having driven so shrewd a bargain. Within the hour old Mother Earth's soft bosom turned to —not limestone, not caliche but to flintrock, the same material as old Doc's heart. Something must be done or we were in for a big losing—chiefly blister fluid and elbow grease. So at thirty minute intervals we would send Bud's little brother, Sonny, around to negotiate a better deal. Sonny, of course, wouldn't ever succeed and we'd accuse him of poor business approach, vacillation, and lack of aggressiveness.

Much more pleasant though much less profitable (since old Doc had relented and paid us twelve) was the painting contract Fush, Jap and Clay Taylor, and I had entered into with the elderly widower anxious to entrap a wife, and speaking of "entrapping," he is the one who paid me the dime for plowing his garden. Said contract called for a coat of white paint on the house, a coat of green paint on the roof, and a coat of red paint on the barn. Although the contract didn't call for it, we put an experimental coat of red paint on one of the old gentleman's fine white hens, which, actually, turned out to be one of ours. I had been too eager to wreak my revenge.

The results so startled and enthralled us we switched over almost exclusively to the study of hen behavior, leaving house and barn to languish and linger. For future students of chicken psychology, the Taylor-Patterson Research and Experimental Laboratories for the study of abnormal behavior in normal fowls, hands down the following pertinent information: A coat of red paint changes completely the white hen's outlook—for the worse. Where once she went singing and cackling pridefully over her work she is now morbid, morose, silent, and seized by sudden anxiety states. She becomes terrified of herself on occasions, said occasions being every time she glances at her reflection in the water trough to see if her comb is on straight or if she is developing pouches. Her image scares the living daylights out of her, scares her to the extent that she seeks immediate solitude under the nearest house or barn, never to absent herself therefromunder until driven out by thirst or hunger. Even then she snatches a few bills full and streaks squawking back to her quarters. She can't eat, she can't roost at night; she starts biting her nails, and her egg production drops off 100 per cent. She assumes her normal personality only after Mother Nature fits her out in a brand new dress. (Which, after all, is a sure sign of normalcy in any female of any species.)

Of further benefit to posterity, perhaps, is the fact that a hen-painting contract not entered into by the party of the first part is not valid, nor that said contract legally entered into will not expire before moulting season. Briefly, the party of the second part, should he expect remuneration, albeit small, from the party of the first part, would do better to plow his garden.

CHAPTER XLVI

Fush, because of his quick, easy transition to the machine age, usually swamped or drove for Papa on his freighting trips to various ranches. This suited me, for after the new wore off (T-Mac was smooth-mouthed, when we got it), I lapsed back into daydreams of becoming a cowboy. Trips to ranches, ordinarily, should have inspired me, but not with them turning more and more to sheep. Too, there was entirely too much heavy lifting and straining involved in hauling freight. (Crossing S crossing on the Pecos we had had to load, unload and reload as many as three times in one trip.) On the other hand when it fell my lot to go along as gate-opener it didn't distress me too much except when our destination was the Tippitt Ranch. Here, I recalled vividly, the wild man hung out, his hideout (in the absence of rafters) being a mesquite thicket just across the Pecos from Government Well.

This time, of all times, it fell my lot to go to this place, of all places. Papa, not completely shed of the horse-drawn age, never choused the T-Mac much beyond wagon speed, possibly for fear the exertion would bring on the heaves. As usual, night overtook us. And, as usual, T-Mac's eyes went out, thus necessitating the making of camp. And, of all places, it had to be Government Well, so named because of its location on the old San Antonio–El Paso mail route. It being so famous as a landmark, everybody—including the wild man—would know of its whereabouts. What's more, it was handier to this wild man's hideout than was Tippitt's headquarters.

"Papa, I can set on the fender and see for you real good. Reckon we better drive on?" I said, trying to sound helpful, resourceful.

"Naw. Better make camp."

I was in hopes that, years removed from the early childhood terrors, my vivid imagination would have lost some of its sharpness. But it was as fresh and as frightening as back in the nester-rafter days. Even so, I eventually dozed off, but with the wild man pictured plain as day in my mind. Around midnight or thereabout I was brought straight up out of the bedroll by a wild, crazy laugh.

"Ha ha ha ha ha-a-a-a-a-a-a-a-ah!" it said. The voice of the wild man exactly as described to me. I was dead certain this was he, because the voice came from up in the windmill tower. Any kid in the abandoned nester-shack country knew that any wild man or woman in his or her right mind wouldn't think of lodging anywhere but in windmill towers, or rafters.

"Hoo hoo hoo ah ha-a-a-a-a-a-ah!," it hollered again. My hair bristled like old Philip's used to when he wanted to fight—only I wanted to run. Trembling as if in a violent chill I elbowed Papa, and in a whisper scarcely audible to myself asked him, "Papa, who's—who's that?" I already knew the answer—the wild man, but I reckon I just wanted to find out his name.

"Hmmmmmmmmmm. What?"

"Who's doin' that crazy hollerin' and laughin' up in the windmill?"

"Jist a old hoot owl."

"No, it ain't either. A hoot owl hoots. Papa, listen!"

"Yes, it is a owl. I'll show you."

"Papa, don't—don't stir 'm up," I whispered, pleadingly, but Papa, rock in hand was walking away from the tower in order to get a better throw. Not risking being caught alone I stuck to Papa like a Siamese twin. Presently he let fly with the rock. If the thing was the wild man he had wings for he flew off into the night. I felt like letting go a crazy laugh myself, I was that relieved. Eleven years in the hoot-owl country, and this was the first owl I ever heard hoot like this. This owl, I reasoned, must have been the wild man's parrot. He had been taught to laugh just like parrots of normal people had been taught to cuss.

CHAPTER XLVII

Despite the glamor and grandeur of the White House we continued to yearn for *thirty-seven* which just might be a home of our own. Besides, $6.oo per month for rent was prohibitive. Consequently, Papa's announcement that he had bought one came as a shock. However, the real bombshell was yet to fall. This home of our own (two homes, actually, *thirty-seven* and *thirty-eight*) turned out to be a couple of shacks set frontier fashion fairly close together with a "dog trot" in between (between which a respectable dog wouldn't trot, the way we kids figured it).

Thirteen now and somewhat increased in both size and sensitivity, I looked upon this humble domicile with extreme loathing. This was a residence unbefitting a judge, and most especially a judge's son. But our varying degrees of scorn, disappointment, disgust, and disgrace affected Papa not one jot nor tittle. His Honor the Judge was still a man living within his means, still not one to put on airs he couldn't afford.

"That's the way he is," Fush pointed out, more in *anger* than in *sorrow*. "If Papa, naked, had his choice between a $1.98 barrel and a $2.oo suit of clothes, he'd turn down the suit and go home in the barrel."

"Straight-out nester shacks," I said to myself, "complete with naked rafters." Here I couldn't restrain a sardonic smile upon recalling Sog's remark relative to number *eighteen*. Now I could go him one better. To inhabit our rafters they would have to be twice as crazy. But not half as crazy as we are, at that.

Naked rafters notwithstanding and a leather latchstring on the slab-board front door (of which I was equally ashamed), the Rankin kids found it no different from the White House. That is to say, "the latchstring was ever out" as far as they were concerned. As a result I began to soften, or rather harden, to it, what with Clay Taylor, Bud Monroe, and we smaller fry putting ourselves in splendid physical fettle chinning and skinning cats on the joists (which we *still* called rafters).

Soon after we moved into this residence-gymnasium, Madge upped and married. Barely sixteen, and after a whirlwind courtship, her marriage astounded and dumfounded Papa, but I figured she figured this was the only alternative to winding up "up in the rafters." Besides, she married Allan Holder, a widely-known widely-traveled rodeo hand. Think of how many miles she could put between herself and these nester shacks.

"If I could find me a famous rodeo woman," I said to myself, "I would go me therefore and do likewise."

What with Gwen only ten and needing to serve a bit more time at apprenticeship, Papa took over the cooking full time. He was a good cook, or had been in his day, but had little time to exploit his talents or regain his touch. His first batch of biscuits would have broken a plate if dropped from any sort of altitude, and his pride was stung. He laid it on the flour, the grease, the clabber, the soda, the baking powder, a bird's nest in the flue, the moon not being right—everything but himself. He even went so far as to blame the crossties and was overheard to mutter, "It ought to be agin the law to cook with anything except mesquite wood."

Despite desperate, frantic experimentation, the biscuits showed no improvement. As a last resort Papa discarded lifelong methods of measurement—a four-finger pinch of this, a sprinkling of that, a smidgin of the other, and resorted strictly to measuring spoons.

Still no improvement. In desperation, not to say dust and ashes, he wrote Madge for counsel. The wait was long and agonizing, not to say indigestion-ridden, since Papa's letter had to trail her back and forth across the broad sweep of the U.S.A. Eventually, her response came, leaving Papa completely vindicated. That was soda in the little baking powder can, and salt in the middle-sized baking powder can. But what he had been using for *soda was the starch!*

This unhappy experience with the starch seemed to have taken the starch out of Papa, literally. It seemed to have destroyed his delicate sense of measurement, stultified his sensitivity for the proper proportion of ingredients. Even after the soda was restored to its rightful place in the proper baking powder can the biscuits showed only slight improvement. Result, cooking came under the complete supervision of Gwen, Papa reserving only the right to continue with the churning.

Although the last couple of generations may laugh me to scorn, I'm here to maintain that churning was one of the higher skills. The talent for churning butter was inherited just as was the talent for music, for poetry, or for creating beauty on canvas. That is to say, it was truly an art—an art at which Papa was a virtual virtuoso. Papa could, in a few graceful strokes, produce a pound or two of the firmest, sweetest substance that ever graced a biscuit or complemented a simmering slab of cornbread. Just as the master (home)-brewmaster of that day knew when his product was ready to "come off" Papa could sense the exact moment when his churning was ready. Even through the thick, crowbar callouses of his hand he could gauge the temperature of the churn. On rare occasions when he did misjudge the temperature, a teeny splash of water from the dipper or teakettle would fix that.

But with Papa out of town, churning was no longer an art—it was an onerous chore—worse than heading maize.

"Paul, it's your turn."

"My turn to what?" feigning innocence.

"Your turn to churn."

"No, it ain't either. It's Gwen's."

"It not done it either. It's Paul's." And it always was.

Then endless battering and splattering, bashing and splashing of that home-made churn dasher up and down, up and down, only to wind up taking our butter out of the glass (with the buttermilk) or dipping little beads of it out with a spoon. But always with an uneasy glance back over the shoulder.

"Papa ever ketches a churnin' turnin' out like this," Fush surmised, "he'll bash somebody in the head with the dasher."

Churning was not only an art with Papa, it was a ritual—an act as sacred as the laying on of hands. We kids were expected to not only talk softly but to tread lightly during the churning ritual. What's more we were to do so under highly sanitary conditions. And he expected no less of himself, refraining completely from Tinsley until that butter was worked, patted and put away in the galvanized cooling pan that sat in the window. What's more it was one of the very, very rare occasions when he removed his hat. Whether this was for further sanitary measures or merely through respect for the calling, we were never to know for certain. Probably the former, Fush reasoned, since the last hide tanning we got resulted from an incident (or rather accident) that occurred during a churning.

The setting was our combination kitchen-diningroom-bedroom and the time was late at night. Papa was at the dining table dexterously wielding his butter paddle (home-whittled and of redolent cedar) over a pan of fresh-churned butter. All of a sudden there came a commotion from the south bedroom, out of which rolled Fush and I fighting. Typical of his tactics he attempted to stifle me with a stale sock and then bolted for the door. Snatching up same I hurled it at the fleeing figure. I aimed to kill him with it, but my aim was poor. The sock landed square on Papa's shoulder. A buzzard lighting thereon couldn't have horrified him more or galvanized him into more action. Faster than a Hickok draw he had us both brought to book and our bottoms batted. The measures he took were extreme, yet sanitary. He carefully laid the butter paddle aside and applied the bare hand.

The curtain comes up exactly four nights later on the same setting, same situation, and almost the same set of circumstances, but a slightly different cast of characters. Fush, cognizant of his propensity for creating crises, thought it expedient to skip a churning or two and had received permission to spend the night with Jap Taylor. The moon, the weather, the temperature, the crockery in the churn, even the broom-handle handle of the dasher—everything—had collaborated tonight for a perfect churning. Now, Papa was plying the butter paddle with loving care. Gwen and I, completely out of harm's way, were down on the floor playing jacks. My turn, and I was about to attempt the very difficult maneuver called "rounding up the strays" (where you have to rake widely-scattered jacks through the "four gates" of your outspread fingers). Consequently, I was going to have to throw the ball 'way high.

Churk!

Slow of wit notwithstanding, I immediately realized why the ball didn't come back down. Instantaneously I analyzed the *Churk* as the sound of a hard rubber ball submerging in a pan of buttermilk (on which surface, and thereunder, still floated ungathered blobs of butter). My next move required no rationalization; it was instinctive, i.e., cringing—in preparation for a paddling. I wasn't prepared, however, for Papa's next move—which was no move at all—just a prolonged, glassy-eyed glare. Sheer grief, pure disbelief, or something, had left him in a catatonic stupor. Even with his voice back he uttered not one word of reproach. However, come daylight next morning we could tell by the compelling urgency with which he cussed at and cranked on the old T-Mac and drove away that he was about to take measures of some sort. Later on he showed up with a stack of lumber—one-by-twelves, two-by-fours, and sundry other scantlings. Summoning all hands he lit in and boxed up an enclosure between the shacks in what turned out to be a diningroom-kitchen. What's more it was a kitchen no bigger than a kitchen range, a kitchen cabinet, a dining table, and two long benches—not big enough even to hurl a stale sock in or play a quiet, polite game of jacks.

I didn't resent the lack of jacks space, but as chief water boy I was bitter at the new kitchen's lack of running water—a facility now enjoyed by practically every household in Rankin except ours.

"The closest we'll ever get to runnin' water," I whined, "is the Pecos." To add insult to injury, the windmill from which I toted water didn't even belong to us but to a neighbor. In return for our keeping it pumping we were welcome to all the water we could use—which was too much, the way I looked at it. Gwen, now the chief cook (and a good one), though only 11 years old, could use more water than three women thrice her age.

CHAPTER XLVIII

What with Fush either swamping for Papa full time, or out on his own, I fell heir to all the chores. In addition to wood chopping, chip gathering, water toting, and some dish washing, I inherited Fush's milking job, but without inheriting Papa's mastery of the cow brute. He had a knack with milk cows just as he had with the by-products thereof. A cow, regardless of how retarded mentally, seemed to understand Papa right off. The first time he said "saw" she sawed and stayed so forever thereafter. Furthermore, she backed her foot at his command and kept it backed, tucked her tail and kept it tucked until he gave her the barnyard equivalent of "at ease." Nor would she ever dare raise the bovine equivalent of two fingers indicating "may I be excused?" as long as Papa was in the same cowpen with her, much less down milking.

On the other hand, my seven years at the "saw" end of a cow left me sadder but no wiser as to bovine behavior. During this length of time I did, however, learn something of the nerve structure of a cow. The nerve ends that terminated in the udder are connected directly to both bladder and bowel. And in case of chapped teats, ganglia leading therefrom control the muscles that switch the tail horizontally to the right.

Perhaps my thwartings stemmed from the fact that our old cow was superior to me in intelligence, or at least she had digested more of Rankin School's reading and arithmetic than I had (which fact almost triggered a stroke in combined Superintendent-Janitor Williams).

"The digestion thereof wasn't so bad," stated Supt.-Janitor Williams, "it was the digestion thereof, therein, and thereon the bookroom floor that set me off."

The Patterson menfolks, all home at the time, received the intelligence of old Dilsey's dastardly deed with varying degrees of emotion. Ralph, Sog, and Fush took it lightly but politely (taking into consideration Supt.-Janitor Williams menacing state of mind). Papa's reaction was acute embarrassment plus a kindred sense of outrage with Mr. Williams. Although professing outrage and shock along with them I was hard put to restrain myself from open rejoicing. Not that I harbored any resentment toward Mr. Williams, I didn't. (However, I figured he should be able to tolerate one time what I had put up with twice a day for seven years.) My secret satisfactions at old Dilsey's doings stemmed from a hostility toward the schoolhouse itself and the humility and embarrassment I had suffered therein.

Burned deep within my memory, constantly and consistently etched there, had been shame at the type of clothes I'd had to wear to school, but what had made Dilsey's doings so soul-satisfying was one incident etched indelibly in my memory. That was the day I had had to attend school barefoot. "Barefooted," and me crowding twelve years old—the biggest barefooted kid in school, and the oldest by two or three years. It wasn't that one pair of shoes was beyond Papa's means; it was that I had overstepped my authority, had bought a pair on credit without first getting Papa's consent. Would that old Dilsey had followed me to school that day (like Mary's lamb)—anything at all to distract attention from my bare feet. The sailor straws only indicated a complete lack of good taste, whereas the bare feet to those who didn't know the circumstances indicated a complete lack of money.

With Prof. Williams placated and gone the big boys had a field day at the expense of me and Papa.

"Papa, you can't blame old Dilsey too much," Ralph pointed out, "recollect how you wouldn't allow her to 'go out' on our premises. Not even in the cowpen."

"Papa, I'd have Paul investigated as an accessory after the fact," Sog put in. "He must've been there milkin' her at the time. Otherwise how would she have got the idea?"

By now Papa was beginning to enter into the spirit of the thing.

"A nasty trick to play on Prof., but you'll have to own up, she's the smartest cow in town."

"How's that?"

"The only cow critter I know of that's learnt the combination to that front gate."

"Not only that," Sog put in, "but she digested more arithmetic in thirty minutes than Fush and Paul have in three years."

Although I was now above the petty retaliations of the Loraine days, I couldn't help but parry this one, "You've done pulled that one once, and it wasn't even funny the first time."

Fush, I could tell, was honing to put in his two-bits worth but dassent for two reasons. One, I could demand an explanation of that hand he injured on Alton Holland's car door three years back (and I had been milking ever since). And, two, he was still considered too young to speak out on such matters.

CHAPTER XLIX

Some fifteen miles east of Rankin in late July of 1923 a bankrupt, long-shot wildcat well blew in and there mushroomed up from the greasewoods flats two oil towns—Texon and Best. (More of Best later, when it's at its worst.) And mushrooming up from these oil towns was considerable romance, thus establishing for Papa a land-office business in the marrying trade. Drillers, tooldressers, oil scouts, rig builders, roughnecks, roustabouts, bootleggers, gamblers, cowboys, mule skinners, truck drivers, and an occasional sheepherder dropped in with their respective prospective brides for Papa to "slap the holy bonds on." Although it pricked Papa's conscience and sense of fair play (he thought the judge's salary should cover such eventualities), these bridegrooms would slip him from a twenty-dollar bill on down, depending upon each's state of sobriety—or stage of inebriety.

Blanche and Madge, on their occasional visits home, were delighted to witness (as required by law) these nuptials, but in their absence it fell the lot of Gwen and myself to stand up with the happy couple. And since nobody ever seemed to get the urge to wed except in the wee small hours, it made for considerable irritability on our part.

"Looks like Blanche and Madge would move back here. They like junk like this," I grumbled.

"Very reason they're not here," Gwen reminded me, though I didn't catch on.

A man of few words, and less experience, Papa's ceremonies were a scant sentence more than asking for the two "I do's." However, he said he was seriously considering tacking on the clause "for drunker, for soberer" along with the "for richer, for poorer." There were times when these weddings were prompted more by shots from the bottle than from Cupid's bow. One night a big tool-dresser interrupted Papa at the part that said: "Do you take this woman to be your lawfully wedded wife?"

"Shay," he said, "haven't I heard that shommers before? Hey! No. Hold on," he exclaimed, a note of sobriety creeping into his tone, "I done got one back down east someplace."

And there was another happy couple who had no sooner finished exchanging vows until they commenced exchanging blows. It all came about by the bride's requesting that the bridegroom carry her to the front gate. Under the circumstances he was doing remarkably well to carry himself. And there was the December-June romance between an attractive young Mexican-American girl and a prominent, prosperous, elderly citizen of that part of town. One evening months before the scheduled date the prospective bride showed up, a rather reluctant bridegroom-to-be on her arm.

"I thought it was August," Papa said, bumfuzzled by such short notice.

"We marry now thees night," she said. "Lately he seek. Maybe so pretty soon die."

Of the scores of drillers, tool-dressers, bootleggers, and cowboys Papa married, my only really enjoyable one was that of a sheepherder. It was a pleasure, especially, because the bridegroom was our old *compadre* Pedro Martinez of the Upland jail days. And Pedro had had the common decency and consideration to get married at a decent hour. What's more this wedding was planned, long anticipated, and Pedro and bride were dressed for the occasion, especially Pedro. He was diked out within an inch of his life. Brilliant yellow, high-topped shoes with pull-on loops in back, which loops served, ingenuously, as holders-off-the-floor of Pedro's overlong pants' legs. The length of these brand new powder-blue trousers was such that they ran horizontal accordion pleats from the pull-on loops upward to Pedro's knees. Powder-blue shirtsleeves in keeping with pants' legs, that is, horizontal accordion pleats running from pink sleeve holders upwards to shoulders. Black bow tie to match mustache but not nearly so widespread. For once there was a part in Pedro's raven locks, dead center and arrow straight, that terminated at the foot of a high black rooster tail, which latter Fush said was already waving "yes" to Papa's forthcoming "Do you take this woman ...?"

Completely smothered in the splendor of Pedro's wedding habiliments was the black-shawled, broad, broad-smiling bride to be. Fact is, I wouldn't have noticed her at all if she hadn't been so closely welded to Pedro.

"Shhhhhhhhh, here we go," Gwen whispered.

"Ahemmmmm," Papa said, "Ahemmmmm, ahemmmmm."

"Why does Papa always clear his throat that-a-way, when it's his head that needs it," Gwen said, nettled at the needless delay.

"What do you mean?"

"I mean he's forgot his openin' remarks as usual and is stallin' for time."

Papa's eye, in search of the place, was dancing frantically on the open book. After a couple of eternities the eye steadied and the voice (in need of steadying) took over. The ceremony was on.

Hub, up from below Sheffield to act as interpreter, did himself proud in two languages, although excited in both. Papa's ceremonies, like his conversation, were limited to the barest essentials, so it wasn't any time until Pedro and fiancee were man and wife.

"Hope old Pedro tries to kiss her," Fush had added the word *tries* believing a kiss through Pedro's mustache an utter impossibility. Evidently Pedro believed likewise for he turned to accept the congratulatory hand of Hub and other well-wishers. Although

Pedro's *adíos* wasn't as sad as the one back in Upland, we hated to see his kind move on. It meant back to those nocturnal nuptials and further inroads on our sleep.

Despite the inroads these impromptu weddings made into our nights' rest I was beginning to look upon them with a degree of tolerance. For one thing, romance itself wasn't as distasteful as formerly but mainly it had improved our financial situation to a marked degree. Now there was a rug or two on the floor, a couple of brand new wooden bedsteads to replace the iron ones and a practically new bureau which we now called a dresser. Finally, to almost equal in elegance the majestic cookstove in the combination kitchen-diningroom was a spanking new coal-burning, silver-nickle dome-top heating stove (to replace the $2.18 sheet steel one) in the parlor-bedroom.

Even so, we still had a long way to go—to the bathroom, especially. And our bathtub was still a number-2. But Papa, county judge notwithstanding, was still a man to live within his means—by all means!

CHAPTER L

What with Papa raking in the exorbitant sum of $1,200 per year as County Judge (plus another $100—which he accepted with qualms—as county school superintendent), plus this booming business in the marrying trade, plus freighting on the side, we were prospering beyond our wildest dreams. Papa, however, not to be stampeded by what he considered a flash in the pan, continued along the even tenor of his ways; still unashamed, unabashed at the "dog trot" home arrangement with its leather thong front door-latch and the naked rafters above the living room.

Constant, strident, and unremitting pressure, however, finally prevailed. Papa ceiled off the rafters and replaced the thong with a bright green cord. However, to let us know he wasn't to be buffaloed he took his own good time about it. What's more, by way of revenge he saw to it that the brunt of the drudgery was done by Fush and me, at which task he drove us unmercifully. But for the ruggedness we had acquired in this rafter calisthenics, the overhead sheet-rocking would have killed us. It would have anyhow on the earlier diet of sowbelly and flour gravy.

"Give a kid an inch, . . ." so it wasn't thirty days until we were harping and carping for even better quarters—porcelain doorknobs, window shades, that sort of thing. It was the oil companies, bless their corporate hearts, that made it possible for us to bring Papa abreast of the times if not quite abreast of his means—and the Joneses. By consistently paying far above Papa's asking price, Gulf, Humble, Magnolia, Ohio, Marathon, were our allies in the eventual prying Papa loose from his dog-trot domain, referred to by some members of the family as *thirty-seven*, and by others as *thirty-seven* and *thirty-eight*. But the oil companies, even in collusion, didn't find Papa a pushover. For example, I delivered to him a $45 check for one day's hauling, and I thought he was going to have Humble Oil Company disenfranchised for squandering—either that or me, his own son, arrested for extortion. You would have thought I had just handed him $45 in bootlegging bribe money.

Finally, seeing as how he couldn't fight the corporations, especially since they were in collusion with his own flesh and blood, Papa made the longest jump, but the shortest move of his career— home *thirty-eight* or *thirty-nine*. The house next door. He bought it lock, stock, and porcelain doorknobs. What's more it had a windmill, cow lot, chicken house, and barn. The house, built in an L shape, consisted of three rooms, an L-shaped gallery on the back and a full length gallery on the front, facing the east. Truly an abode beyond our wildest dreams. Mine, Fush's, and Gwen's, that is, not Papa's.

In a fit of reckless abandon he lit in and built onto the west end of it, not a shed room or lean-to but an addition that blended in perfectly with the rest of the house. If the sheet-rocking of the shack was hard going, Fush and I hadn't seen anything yet—sawing scantlings, setting joists, shagging shingles, from sun to sun and beyond. As proud as we were of the pitched roof at first, we wound up whimpering to each other of this diabolical plot of Papa's.

"This-a-way he figgers we're more apt to slip off and kill ourselves," I whined to Fush.

"If he don't work us to death first," Fush gritted, his reply made more venomous by shingle nails clenched between his teeth. Speaking of between the teeth, Papa took the bit and had Ralph wire the entire house for electric lights, back porch, front porch, and all. Moreover, he lit in and had us box in the bottom half of the back porch and then finish out the top with heavy canvas, on the order of wagon sheeting or tarpaulin. We wanted to point out to him that everybody, who was anybody, would have screened it. But knowing his reply would have been: "Aw, a feller can't go back on his raisin'," we let it ride. Besides, we weren't sure yet that this whole house wasn't a brief dream—with a long nightmare of work to it.

As if this weren't enough to supply conversation pieces for the next forty years he hauled off and bought a brand new bedroom suite, and a carpet of sorts for the combination parlor, living room, bedroom, den. Then he bought a carpet for Gwen's room. (I couldn't kick. Somebody had brought me a goat hide for my bedside on the south end of the back porch.)

But give kids an inch, . . . This time, however, we let up, seeing as how every improvement, every new comfort, put more callouses on our hands. And, after all, from all outward appearances the place was a residence befitting a man of Papa's stature, worthy of the calling which Judge Patterson now pursued.

CHAPTER LI

Just as Papa's ambition to live within his means remained unswerving, so did mine to become a cowboy. Judging from Fush's everyday behavior, his resolve was likewise steady and constant—a resolve to follow in the boot tracks of Sog, of Papa, and of Papa's trail-driving Uncle Dave. In fact he may have harbored ambitions of hitting the rodeo trail like brother-in-law Allan Holder, or like our bronc-riding Uncle Fisher, for he and Jap Taylor and Alton Holland had only recently topped off a bunch of broncs in the stock pens. The rodeo circuit? Not for me. Too rugged even for me to daydream about. Not only the monstrous, man-eating horses and bulls but the alternate periods of feast and famine, of stuff and starve, that rodeo people went through with. Of late my wood-hauler's, coal-scuttler's appetite had to have regular and steady attention.

"Fush," I told him, "you're on your way. You've done rode some pitchin' horses."

"Humph, none of 'em could a throwed off a wet saddle blanket."

"What kind you want then, pure outlaws like Sog rides into town sometimes?"

"Absolutely. And I want 'em outside. Not in no pen."

"But like Papa says, you're still jist a button," I said, dodging. "However," I said reassuringly, "purty soon you can choose your callin'."

Not three weeks from that day he had set his life's course, had chosen his profession—barbering! Incredibly and ironically he had upped and enrolled in a Dallas barber college.

"Right out of a clear sky," was my only explanation for it.

Fush's bizarre behavior triggered all sorts of traumas in our family, especially as regards the noble occupation of the range. Ralph hung up his saddle and enrolled in an electrical school in Chicago, and Sog called for his time at the Y's and rode in to swamp for Papa and do oil-field work. A sad and alarming state of affairs. The first time in at least sixty years that the cowboy profession wasn't represented by some branch of the Pattersons. Somebody would have to do something about it. The somebody would have to be *me*. And the *something* would have to be other than day-dreaming.

But formidable barriers lay ahead. First, it would be like crashing Devil's Island to get free of the mean and menial tasks Papa had me chained to. Second, incredible that anybody would hire me if I were available. Except for minor incidents my cowboy experiences had been restricted chiefly to the printed page. Finally, and the greatest obstacle of all, could I, with my poor co-ordination and timid spirit, hold down a cowboy job? Sog could. And my co-ordination was better than his, what with his having to jump from childhood right into manhood and on horseback. No chance to gain action and agility afoot. Yes, my agility was better than Sog's, but where we came to the forking of the trails was in timidity of spirit. When it came to anything in the cowboy line Sog's timidity of spirit was about like that of a lion or a grizzly bear. There was the difference.

I couldn't help but search carefully back through his past, seeking some clue, some helpful handle to grasp from his experiences— anything to enhance my chances to get on "study" with some of the bigger outfits. A perusal of his past revealed formidable obstacles I'd have to overcome if I expected to ride the rocky trail that he had.

CHAPTER LII

In retrospect it seems incredible how impervious, or at least indifferent, I remained to my surroundings. Here was more action per capita per square mile than ever before, early cowboy and Comanche days not excepted, yet to my way of thinking merely oil patch shenanigans, perpetrated afoot. Action wasn't action, excitement wasn't excitement unless done on horseback, or perpetrated, at least, by former horsebackers.

What with Ralph and Fush lost forever to the noble calling and Sog backsliding from time to time, one would think I would succumb to the new age. No. No, indeed. That cowboy-for-to-be call continued to ring in my ears like the siren's song. Mine was a chronic case of romanticism, of idealism. Nay, not a chronic case, possibly a terminal one.

"Sog, how can I ever qualify as a cowboy haulin' wood?" I asked in a tone reminiscent of the Loraine days.

"Why, that's qualifyin' you right where it counts most—where the saddle fits. Haven't you ever heard how tough a wood hauler's is?"

"Yeah, but a man's got to be tough all over."

"Number 7 coal scoop'll take care of that."

"It won't teach me to ride."

"No. But it'll make you bounce easier. And harder to bruise."

Ordinarily Sog's incurable optimism was communicable but somehow I found this case nontransmittable. In fact, it was having an adverse effect, so I moved off to seek solace in solitude, to reassess my chances, to reevaluate my experiences. The picture looked bleak. That trail trip to Old Ma's was of no value whatsoever—a stumbling, starving herd was no comparison to the snuffy, snaky, sassy critters of these rainier times. And the week-end works with Jake Massingill, Cap Yates, and Cody Bell would actually hinder my chances were a would-be employer to look into my qualifications. Jake's, Cap's, and Cody's hiring me in the first place was more from softheartedness than from necessity—they merely wanted to grant me respite from the coal cars and the crosstie runs.

Most of my work with Jake had been afoot—crowding steers into the dehorning chutes and keeping the branding fire hot. At the former I was my usual inept self—critters too snaky and too handy with either end. But at the latter I proved to all (and too soon) and for all time that I hadn't lost that incendiary touch of the Taylor place days. Jake had taken the cowboys on a drive and sent me, Lee Lane, and Uncle Jimmy O'Bryan to the house to fire up the kitchen range. We not only fired up the kitchen range; we fired up the kitchen as well. And, subsequently, the whole house. Just as I had told Papa some ten years previous, "It wasn't my fault, cross my heart." Neither was it Lee Lane's or Uncle Jimmy's.

From the corrals we saw that we had "overbuilt," but it was too late. As a throwback to the wilder cattle days, the windmill was two hundred yards from the house and, consequently, useless in an emergency such as this. But Uncle Jimmy had continued to battle the blaze long after we realized the cause was lost, whereas Lee and I had begun to take it more than philosophically. Lee was a calm customer around fires, be they house or prairie, calmer here than during the Upland prairie blaze, however, for he didn't risk a corduroy jacket.

Of the two riding jobs I had with Jake, one ended in utter failure and the other in near tragedy. The first time I got lost on drive (an unpardonable sin), and the second time I stepped off a lively Indian pony without first loosening my foot in the stirrup. The instant my right foot hit the ground I realized that my left one was hung. And so did Bravo. Wheeling violently to the right he was fixing to strew greenhorn accessories across the rolling plains when he collided with the tank dump and fell, thus allowing me time to extract my foot from the stirrup. The pale, set faces of the cowboys made me realize the gravity of the situation. Jake, with far more patience than I had ever credited him, put me back on the ground for the rest of the works.

"Damn, Paul. Safer for you—and for everybody—if you'll jist stay afoot. Now with the house burnt down maybe you can't do too much harm!"

Cap Yates had hauled me out occasionally and taken infinite pains to teach me the knack, but his luck was no better than Jake Massingill's. He cut me the gentlest horse on the ranch but I still couldn't mount out until Cap had gone through the process first. Not just at topping-off time in the morning but all through the day. Then there was the time Cody Bell had let me and Fush help him deliver his mules—some hundred head and as snaky as blacktailed deer. With Cody in the lead and us on swing and flank (there weren't any drags) we coursed them into the Rankin stock pens without spilling a one. This should be recommendation enough, but then I recollected that Cody had told us later that my mount, old Chevrolet, had died soon after that trip.

And there was the time Hal Holmes and I were delivering a couple of young horses that Arthur Schnaubert and Billy Rankin had broken for Hal's dad. We were loping along, Hal keeping a sharp eye on his mount and I admiring my shadow. Nothing to worry about, I figured, locked in securely under the eighteen inch swell fork of Sog's saddle. All of a sudden my colt swallowed his head and stacked me, face first, saddle and all onto the gravelly road.

"What on earth happened to your face?" was the stock question for weeks thereafter. Hard put as I was to answer in my own embroidering style I stuck strictly to Sog's approach.

"Gravel rash," I explained.

Then I would relate briefly and modestly the story, careful to throw in the fact that the girt broke. Then along came Oscar Schnaubert, a bronc rider of some renown with the following observation.

"That'll learn a feller to stay on 'em, won't it, Paul?"

"It'll learn a feller to stay off of 'em, too." I replied, drawing quite a laugh. Just as I was careful to add about the girt breaking, I was equally as careful to omit the fact that originally this was Sog's witticism. After sober reflection I realized this incident wouldn't serve as a recommendation either. The would-be employer might interpret it as an application for a bronc riding job. Lord forbid!

Rifle the recesses of memory to a fare thee well I couldn't come up with a single incident that would recommend me. Well, there was the time I had delivered, single-handed, afoot, and alone 183 head of lambs for Jim Robbins and didn't spill but one.

"Better keep quiet about that," Sog advised me. "More successful a feller is as a herder, less apt he is to land a cowboy job."

CHAPTER LIII

The freedom and independence for which Mama bided her time and then achieved that July day in 1919 meant more to her than we had realized. Seven years had passed and she still hadn't come home. Ralph and Sog, on their way to Kansas with cattle trains, had dropped in on her briefly while the stock was being watered and fed there in Altus, Oklahoma.

"Why, my, my, my. How are you chillern?" She was delighted to see them and anxious to hear about everybody (except Papa). The visit was pleasant and relaxed until the boys broached the subject of Mama's coming home.

"What home?" she asked cynically. Sarcasm and bitterness weren't in her make-up except where Papa was concerned. But the mere mention of his name set her off and unleashed a facet of her nature that verged on violence.

"We got a pretty good old shack now," Ralph said.

"May not have when you get back. Did I ever tell you chillern how he traded off a five-room house in Midland—a fine big home..."

"Oughta been. He traded four sections of land for it!" Ralph wedged in quickly, realizing that from here on, until Mama had poured out twenty years of grievances, interruptions would be few and far between.

"Twenty-nine moves in all—jumping from pillar to post, from post to pillar, each place worse than the one before. Lived in a half dugout one time. And in a one-room shack with a dirt floor, and in tents and by the roadside in camps and on the road. Three times that I know of we've been burnt out. You chillern remember when the Taylor place burned and we didn't save anything hardly at all. One time over in Sterling County a cyclone hit. As luck would have it it didn't hurt the house much but tore up the chicken house and buggy shed. But living with your Papa was like a cyclone anyhow. I ever tell you chillern about the time he sat on the windmill till two in the morning with a gun? Says "I'm lookin' for wolves." I told you chillern to go on to bed but "I'm going to keep an eye on him." I thought he was waiting to kill us all. I knew a man in Coryell County one time . . .

"He, your Papa, was driving from Garden City to Big Spring working old Buck and Brownie to a white-topped hack. I told him I says, 'don't drive into that train.' He drove within an inch of it. John, you was three years old. I jerked the lines out of his hands. Had a premonition next time and kept a horse tied to the hack for riding purposes. Your Papa drove and I rode the horse and he whipped the team over a hill and out of sight. Wouldn't stop. Five miles to Big Spring and I told a man along the road, 'My husband and three chillern have run off and left me and I can't find my way on in. The man rode with me all the way to your Grandma Patterson's. I had a hemorrhage and came in an inch of dying. Things like that.

"One time he started to choke me over the coffee and once was about to hang me with a rope. I said to myself, said, 'I'm dying before my time.' About that time you, little John, toddled in and he dropped the rope and walked off. Providence. Some people had it out that he might hang his own chillern."

"Times there, Mama, when we needed it . . ."

"He was that way. High-tempered. When he came up here after Paul and little Gwen he seemed to have cooled down some. But his coolings don't last. When they said, 'Mama, won't you please come back with us,' a woman here at the rooming house said 'she's between two fires.' And your Papa said to Gwen, 'you come home with me and I'll buy you a dolly,' and he said to me 'you can come too if you want to.' No, sir. Life with your Papa is too risky, too uncertain, too jumping out of the frying pan into the fire. Never!" Here the flow of words was replaced by a flow of tears. Abruptly Mama had ended the visit, excusing herself to go about her boardinghouse duties.

"Sog, you know her better than I do; will she ever come back?" Ralph asked.

"No. You can tell by the way she tells her tale, straight on through, without the usual back tracks, side roads, and extra experiences she used to throw in."

The landlady, at first a bluff, gruff character, turned out a kindly soul after she had convinced herself that the sons of a beast such as Papa were not spawn of the devil. However, it took the combined sincerity and wits of both boys to convince her that Papa wasn't the devil himself.

"We know your mother may not be quite right in her mind but in many ways she's got the rest of us skinned forty ways from Sunday. A kinder, more trusting heart I never saw in a human being. And where the rest of us see the world goin' to hell in a high lope, to her tomorrow is allus gonna be better than today. The lion is gonna lay down with the lamb, so to speak. A pity she had to live in want and fear of her life all them years."

"What do you mean, fear of her life?"

"Well, your Pa allus fixin' to hang her. Things like that."

"Shoot. Papa was just hoorawin'."

"Your mother don't lie."

"Of course not. To her it's the gospel truth. But did you ever tell Mama a joke? Or play a little prank on her? Well, don't. Her joker was put on backwards."

"But he did choke her, didn't he?"

"Positively not," Ralph said. "You tell her, Sog. He raised you."

"Papa manhandle Mama? No. Trigger-tempered, yes. And rough on balky teams and stubborn milk cows. But he never laid a finger on Mama. I swear it. And one time I saw her spit in his face."

"Well, he could have done somethin' for her that time she laid so long at death's door with childbed fever."

"What more could he do—after eighteen heifer yearlins, ever' hoof he owned? But we ain't gettin' nowhere arguin'. How's she doin' now?"

"Drifts around a right smart. But always comes back. I worry sick over her."

The boys handed the landlady a couple of $20 bills. "Looks like she could use some money."

"Misuse it, you mean. I wouldn't dare give all of this to her at once. Money means absolutely nothing to her—except as somethin' to loan or to give to some needy soul or to some sorry son of a gun with a sad story. Worst part about it is she can't tell the needy from the sorry, and it's generally the sorry that winds up with the big end of her wages. But I'll warantee you one thing; she'll be the last one to fret over it. Tomorrow is goin' to be better. And the next day better still. Still and all, boys, if she was my mother I'd take her home."

"Supposin' you tell her that," Ralph said, assuming, and rightly, that this was one of the very few people with influence over Mama.

"I see what you mean. But keep in touch with her."

"We'll stop back by on our way home. On the eight o'clock southbound next Friday evenin'."

Ralph made the mistake of telling exactly when, for Mama was nowhere to be found. She wasn't about to run the risk of being high-pressured by relatives, friends, or acquaintances into terminating seven years of freedom, of risking an interruption (even temporarily) of that "total independence."

CHAPTER LIV

Now that the oil boom had lapped, in earnest, over into Upton County our next-door neighbors, the John F. Lanes began to get up in the money. Mr. Lane, a friend of years standing, tried to arrange for Papa to improve his circumstances by offering him a block of acreage at rock bottom prices, and on easy terms to boot. But forty acres at $10 per acre! Why, that was $400, equivalent in Papa's eyes to the national debt!

"No, John. But much oblige. A man hadn't ought to overjump hisself and try to live above his means," Papa told him.

The Patterson fortune would have to accrue by the long, hard, agonizing route, a number 7 scoopful at a time, by loadings, un-loadings, and reloadings, via the lurch and scotch method.

"There went my million," Sog said, but without rancor.

"Mine too," I added and likewise with an amazing lack of bitter-ness. Riches were only secondary. My primary purpose in life was to be a cowboy, where the action was. And prospects for the fruition of this dream were brighter than ever before.

With summer at hand, the slack season for wood and coal, and Sog to truck for Papa, the first barrier was removed. There were still formidable stumbling blocks, however—my poor showing here-tofore, my aversion (if not downright allergy) to air exhaled through the noisy nostrils of a bronc, my lack of recommendations, and so on. But politics, plus a friendship of lifelong standing, might just remove that final obstacle. The lifelong friendship with Lee Lane might just do the trick. Old Lee and I had been through flood and fire (both house and prairie) together. Yes sir, Lee, now moving up and spreading out fast in the cow business, was the man to see.

Incredibly, he hired me. But it was to be on a thirty-day trial basis. As it turned out the trial proved too rigorous—both for me and for Lee. Lee was kept too busy running horses loose with saddles, and I was too busy walking to get any riding done. Without Sog's rigid adherence to Cowboy Code 1, I was only too happy to foot it home in peace and safety, when a Bar L threw me, which was far too frequently. First it was old Fal and then kid brother J's pet horse Friday and then old Ranger twice and finally that miserable critter Dirt Dauber.

"Damn, Paul," Lee said, more in pity than in anger, "it looks like one keeps you in the air all time."

"It ain't the in-the-air part that bothers me, Lee, it's that hittin' the ground."

So, in order not to risk rending that lifelong bond of friendship asunder we agreed to terminate our agreement.

Humiliating for one to have to hang up his (or rather his brother's) saddle after only thirty days, as compared to Papa's thirty years. It had its brighter aspects, however. Henceforth and forever I could stand around and tell the boys how "once in the saddle I used to go dashing; oh, once in the saddle I used to be gay, . . ."

Incredible as it may seem, I hadn't more than finished my exciting episode with old Fal, until Billy Rankin came along and hired me. "Bless old Billy," I said to myself, half-choked up with emotion, "only reason he hired me was because he feels sorry for me, like Jake and them did. Doggone it. I don't want nobody hirin' me just because they feel sorry for me."

I should have been greatly relieved to learn that Billy hadn't hired me because he felt sorry for me, but instead, I wound up sorry for myself. No sooner had we set foot on his spread than he pointed me out a half mile of solid rock—into which were to be sunk a half mile of post holes. Not that I expected lots of riding, right at first. Neither did I expect so much standing and stooping, and so little walking between holes.

Before the long slow sun of that first day had sunk I had long since been seized with the druthers—whether I druther be bent over a number seven breathing softcoal dust or leant over a fourteen-pound crowbar breathing flintrock dust. Maybe that old boxcar was 120° in the shade, but it *was in the shade*. Maybe a 75 pound crosstie did feel like 275 coming up a steep bank, but at least you had a feeling of accomplishment, of getting somewhere. But here, a ringing, singing, stinging blow of that crowbar loosened no more than enough dust to sting the lungs. Eventually, as is nearly always the case, things began looking up. Just when I felt that one more ring of that crowbar against my eardrums; one more sting of it against my blood blisters and I'd "by damn call for my time," Billy rode up and said, "Paul, drop your crowbar and come with us. We're goin' up on King Mountain and pick up a couple of broncs I swapped Buck Harmon out of."

Back at the house Bill Wyatt was penning a half dozen or so ponies.

"Horseback job at last," I said in the barest of whispers, for fear of frightening off this flimsy dream.

"Horseback" wasn't quite accurate, for in among the horses was a little red mule, too small to be seen from a distance.

"Paul, you'll ride old Colorow here. From what I hear you ain't had too much luck with horses. So, we'll start off on somethin' easy—say, like a mule."

Incredible, now, that a Blanche-type premonition didn't warn me, or that the wild-mule episode hadn't flashed before me, at least. But at the time Billy's suggestion sounded not only logical but safe, since a mule is half burro and a burro can't begin to pitch like a horse. I should have recalled the Upland-mule episode, seen a premonition, or at least smelled a mouse when they started saddling old Colorado (pronounced colorow). It took Billy, his wife Dolly (strong as any cowboy), and Bill Wyatt all three to buckle my kak on. Then it took them plus old Peeant, the snubbin' horse to ear him down for me to mount out. Had my premonitioner been functioning even at half speed, it would have taken all hands to put me aboard, but I stepped across without a qualm.

Billy was right, old Colorow made a few springy, easy goat-jumps which I weathered with ease. Flushed with victory and feeling like a cowboy I hollered "turn him out." Colorow was reluctant to leave hearth and home, but once persuaded by the double of a rope wielded dexteriously by Billy, he moved out with a free-going gate that was easy as rocking in the parlor. And on the rough mountain trail he was nimble as a cat. "Only thing is," I thought to myself, "I wisht he'd pitch with me—if it's no harder'n he did a while ago."

Whether old Colorow read my thoughts or he was suddenly taken with a homing instinct, I'll never know. But before I could gather my wits—and the saddle horn—that little red devil had kicked my feet out of the stirrups and was speeding homeward with the stride of Dan Patch. For a mule overcome by the homing instinct his zigzaggy actions seemed crazy at first. Crazy like a fox. He was assuming this course in an effort to hang me on a mesquite, for each time he whizzed under one he kicked my feet from the stirrups. Every effort to stop or turn him proved not only futile but hazardous since I needed both hands on the saddle horn. "Why was I trying to stay aboard such a fool anyhow?" was the first thought that occurred to me. Suddenly it also occurred to me how unerring, how accurate a mule is with his hind feet (finally, dang it, visions, or rather apparitions of wild mules chasing me, and old Heave Ho kicking me through a stall wall).

And with this premonition a compelling urge—and a need to get down a minute. With this urge came a secret hope that old Colorow would wheel and bolt. Or make remounting so difficult (without kicking me in the belly) that either Billy or Bill would be forced to take him. No such luck. For reasons known only to God and a mule, he didn't move out of his tracks. Until I threw a leg across, that is. The second my seat hit the saddle and my right foot caught the stirrup he kicked both of my feet out of the stirrups and commenced clearing out mesquite with me.

Instead of jumping out from under me, planting both feet in my belly and having done with it, he kept jumping back under me so as to have something with which to tear off limbs—mine or the mesquites, according to which gave way first. Brush eventually cleared, and me still aboard (but blinded, bruised, bleeding, and busy riding) he headed due south at a dead run—right for the rimrock, which was thirty to sixty feet straight down, according to where you took it. Much mindful of this fact, I pulled old Colorow's head clean around in my lap and anchored it there, dallying a rein around the saddle horn. But it altered his course not one jot, nor checked his momentum not one tittle. And sixty feet of sheer precipice yawned not five jumps ahead.

"God, now it's all up to Thee—I've been an awful good boy!" I added hopefully. Simultaneously, with the conclusion of my prayer old Colorow's ears came from a-straddle of my nose, and there was a harsh skidding sound. I opened my eyes enough to observe old Colorow's outthrust front feet slide to a stop a scant foot short of the rimrock edge. Reeling in the saddle like the legendary Billy Venero with seventeen Apache arrows in him, I reclosed my eyes and offered up thanks to God.

In these few momentous and prayerful seconds a strange transformation had come over the mule too. Once I had the strength to lift the reins, he responded like a polo pony. I tiptoed him from the cliff just as Billy and Bill loped up.

"You ok, Paul?" Billy asked casually—too dang casually. I mustered the strength to nod my head in the affirmative.

"I knew old Colorow wouldn't hurt you. You see," he went on, "a mule's too smart to hurt hisself."

Volumes wouldn't have held my rebuttals to this crack, had I had the breath to reply.

"You know, though. Old Colorow must of realized he'd gone too far, Paul. You notice how he squalled out like a panther, there at the edge of the rimrock?"

I didn't consider a reply. Just as well they didn't know it was me. They soon, and lightly, dismissed this "death rides the rimrock" experience of mine, and we rode along wrapped in silence. I was too weak—too spent for words, but my imagination was a-buzz and a-hum. Though Colorow was saddling along submissively, obviously apologetic for what he'd done, I couldn't dismiss the premonition (dang its late-arriving hide) that he was fixing to do something else dastardly.

"Mule's too smart to hurt hisself" Billy had said. A grim, bitter smile played the length of my pallid lips as rebuttal after rebuttal paraded through my thoughts. How about the JM mules who nearly ran themselves to death trying to catch us kids? How about the time old Whitey carried me straight at what could have been the JM ghost? How about the time that blue mule brayed, giving Buffalo Bill's position away to the Indians? How about the time over in Old Mexico when a Texas Ranger's mule wheeled and ran right square in amongst the enemy? How about old Heave Ho?

Old Colorow's long ears flopped forward, derailing my long train of rebuttals. Little did I dream old Colorow was preparing me another rebuttal—the daddy of them all.

"Looks like a trapper, or somebody, coverin' up his bed," Billy was saying. "Let's us ride by there and . . ." Colorow took the words out of Billy's mouth, the bits between his own teeth and wheeled in that direction, heading out at a high lope. I didn't take issue with him as I knew I'd be wasting my strength—a strength I would need going back down that mountain.

All of a sudden there was a sharp, singing whine overhead, and up ahead a loud report. A man was shooting our way.

"Come back, Paul. Come back," Billy and Bill were yelling. As if

I weren't ripping both arms from their sockets trying to do that very thing. I had Colorow's head lapped plumb around to his tail, and his eyes meeting mine. But it neither altered his course nor the smirking expression on his face—like a jackass eating prickly pear. A gyroscope under his tail couldn't have held him truer to his course. Events were taking place much faster than my reflexes, but a sharper whine and a louder report told me to switch tactics. With superhuman strength I jerked that mule's head back in front of my face—for a breastwork. If it was one tenth as hard as I figured, it was bulletproof.

"Looky here, God. I'm all Thine again." More or less resigned now, as one will be in a hopeless situation, I crouched there waiting for that other shot—the unerring one—to knock me out of the saddle. It didn't come. *Now*, I thought dimly, as I felt old Colorow sliding to a stop. Reckon the feller just wants to make sure. But still no crashing, numbing thud. So I chanced a glance to determine the delay. There leaning against a barrel was a bearded man. He was frisking me with a sharp eye, but his rifle was no longer at the ready.

"Much oblige, God. Again," my voice and soul cried out.

"I'm makin' whiskey—and a little beer on the side—so I jist dropped a couple over you to skeer you around . . . "

"Man, you shore wasted at least one shot, then," I said, my throat dry.

"I first thought 'now there's a gally son—but then I seen yore mule'd cold-jawed. They'll do it ever' time."

"You know," I butted in, "if I thought you'd stood a chance of hittin' this anvil-headed son of a beast I'd a invited a couple more shots."

"You look like you need a drink," the bootlegger said, walking over and throwing the big tarp off several barrels of brew in the process. He handed me a tin cup and I gulped down a batch of the fermenting liquid. A man that light on the trigger might likewise have a supersensitive sense of outraged hospitality. "Fine stuff," I lied, disappointed it didn't have the kick of a mule and thus blot out the thoughts of one.

Under mule stress and strain I had forgotten Bill and Billy who were huddled out a ways, obviously holding a council of war. When I signaled, they came loping up, faces grim under their wide hats.

"Light, fellers. Drinks on the house," said the bootlegger, amiably. They too were quick to sample his product and compliment its excellence, which was also their way of avowing absolute secrecy.

This bootlegger, "shades of the prison house" notwithstanding, turned out to possess a likable disposition. Yes, even lovable, for he took a shine to the treacherous Colorow, allowing the critter free leeway about camp plus all the brewery by-products he could eat. Disgusting!

Harrowing though the day had been perhaps it was getting me somewhere. When Billy asked if I intended to ride Colorow home I said, "N-O, no. Hell, no." And my voice must have carried a most authoritative ring, for he swapped mounts without so much as one word of back talk.

Back at the ranch we got word that Bud Barfield, Clarence Shannon and Hugh Gillispie, McCamey's deputy had just killed two bank robbers in a shoot-out behind the Rankin bank building in the dead hours of the morning. (So, ho hum. What if they'd had to go through what I had been through in the last 24 hours? Safe though it would be in comparison to my experiences, I was somehow thankful that Bud had gotten Ralph and Sog to stay a night or two in the bank, just in case.)

This most harrowing of experiences wrought other marked changes in me. The following Sabbath found me in attendance at Rankin Community Church, where a reasonably skilled lip reader could have gauged the magnitude of my gratitude.

"Lord, Thou hast delivered me twice lately in one hour's time. And in case Thou hast to make it thrice, here am I."

As regards that chronic and terminal compulsion to become a cowboy, quite possible now that it wasn't terminal, or even chronic, for I was more than content to reenroll in school that fall, yes, and condescend to accept a job as assistant janitor of the school. After all, if scavenging wasn't beneath Papa's dignity, sanitary engineering should not be beneath mine.

CHAPTER LV

Canvassed porches, pitched roofs, carpets, porcelain doorknobs, bedroom suite, heater to match the elegance of the lordly cookstove, electric lights—everything we said Papa would never, never have any truck with was now a reality, closer than hands and feet. Now there was speculation, even wagering among us kids, that even though our life style had changed radically, our style of dress never would. And, if there was ever to be a change in our mode of dress Papa would be the last to give in. Even then the change would be imperceptible. Incredibly, Papa was the first, and the change was radical.

Pressure of politics, influence of affluence, tempo of the times, choice of companions? Whatever it was, only God and Papa knew, neither of which was talking. Anyhow, early one morning in late March of 1927 Papa got up and put his pants on before he did his hat, which should have struck us as peculiar. What did strike us as peculiar, however—very peculiar indeed—was the fact that, this time, Papa carefully creased his Stetson before putting it on. So stupefied, so absorbed in Papa's creased hat we were that we failed to take note of other peculiar goings on. We had but to lower our eyes a notch and we could have beheld another marvel—his tying himself a necktie and donning a coat to match his pants! And roving on down, the unbelieving eye could have beheld him stepping into a pair of "blacked" shoes.

What's more, Fush could have told us (but was probably sworn to secrecy) that Papa had commenced getting a barbershop shave every few days. And had gone to keeping the down-sweeping corners of his mouth completely clear of Tinsley tracks.

Whether creased hats, neckties, and blacked shoes, gave him ideas or whether they gave ideas to someone else, we'll never know. But around sunup on May 1, 1927, in walked Papa with a brand new bride on his arm. Maybe neither of the above was the case. Maybe he just got tired of being always the bride's *mater* and never the bride's mate. Nevertheless, it was for the Pattersons the close of an age.

EPILOGUE

Papa, at ninety-seven and two-thirds, made his forty-fifth and last move October 17, 1966, without ever having seen a dark day, without having admitted it, that is. Considering the fact that out of these ninety-seven years, only two hours (the last two) were spent in a hospital, his days *were* easy.

His prescription for longevity, as quoted on his ninety-third birthday was, "Keep your bowels open and your mouth shut." Sage advice from a man for whom the course of true love never did run smooth, even with his second bride. Nor did the rugged trail he always seemed to pick up ever smooth out. Resigning the judge-ship in 1929 he bought a small farm in Palo Pinto County. Shortly thereafter he and his bride burned out (he for the fourth time) and were forced to live under a tree for three months. He bought a smaller farm, starved out and bought a smaller one still.

Eventually he was reduced to a home and garden patch in Mineral Wells, which patch he continued to cultivate until the age of ninety-six. After that he was reduced to walking for exercise (twenty blocks a day), wisecracking with the neighbors and news-paper reading for diversion. Television wasn't his life style except for the news, weather, and Festus on Gunsmoke. "Ol' Festus puts me in mind of so many ol' fellers I've knowed."

Though he didn't die with his boots on—he hadn't worn them

since his cowboy days—he died exactly as he would have preferred it; hat within arm's length and a plug of Tinsley even nearer.

Mama moved on at ninety-one and a half, still looking toward tomorrow as the best, brightest, most opportunity-filled day yet. Even though she hadn't walked a step in twenty-one years, tomorrow she would be up selling thimbles and needles and notions like hotcakes to a thimble-needle-notion-starved public. Though bedfast in body she could still lay claim—and justifiably so—to a completely unfettered imagination which continued to roam restless and free. Without ever becoming aware of it, she had contracted a terminal case of the go-yonders from Papa. Along with the completely unfettered imagination went that total independence of spirit which remained a part of her to the end. Never at any time did she ask anything of anybody, most especially of a Patterson. Which is a far better record than her sixth child could boast. No charity doles, just a few donations, and there were times when I found a loan indispensable.

Ralph's conversion from cowboy to oil patcher proved to be the death of him (or so I used to like to think). He made his last move almost forty years before Papa did (1928) when a .38 caliber pistol fell from a T-Model, discharged, and shot him through the neck. Something of a horizon hunter himself he was ever heeding the siren song of "somewheres else." But the siren song of the oil booming town of Jal, New Mexico, proved his last.

Blanche, who only a few pages back was too young to mother us smaller kids, is already a great-grandmother in Sheffield, Texas. Characteristic of the Patterson breed she still has a zest for living but with a certain degree of solemnity so lacking in the rest of us. Her mail reads, "Mrs. H. A. Holmes."

Sog, at sixty-eight, is still ahorseback off and on—off and on both literally and figuratively. That is to say, he suffered a severely strained back and wrenched hip at sixty-seven and a broken shoulder at sixty-eight. All this plus his upper teeth knocked out at fifty-seven, in addition to countless minor accidents and the two very serious ones of his early manhood. Although he has begun to turn down the roughest broncs he has yet to turn down somebody with a sad, sad story.

As was the case with many cowboys of his day, marriage came rather late in life. Fortunately it was to a lady of like liberal spirit and generous heart. Since she owns a ranch and is an astute, hard-working woman with more financial means than he has ever been accustomed to, money is far easier to come by (and it continues to go just as easily). Nowadays, thanks to a generous wife and a kind fate, John Patterson is riding his own string of horses and is "shore enough on *study*."

Madge, now Mrs. E. L. Howell of Austin, was at Mama's beck and call during the latter's last years. That total independence of spirit didn't preclude Mama's asking a Patterson to run errands to a fare thee well.

Fush, more or less the hero of this piece and onetime man of action, quietly plies his barber's trade in McCamey, the town that sprang up wild and willing out of the greasewoods back in '26. Though strange his choice of vocations, even stranger was his choice of hobbies, especially after what he and I went through with above and beneath the rafters of *thirty-six*, *thirty-seven* and then *thirty-eight*. Even after his having denounced so vehemently through clenched and shingle-nail-gripping teeth the carpenter calling, he chose it and cabinet making as a hobby. The first thing one notices about his carpentry and cabinet shop is the roof. It has a sensible pitch, an almost flat, lean-to style. Something a man couldn't possibly slide off of.

Gwen, Mrs. H. D. Shaw, is the only Patterson left in Rankin, which great and noble city was once the capital of the universe around which all other stellar bodies revolved. A modest, unassuming girl she isn't likely to claim the title of *youngest living champion covered wagon mover of the world*—which she is.

As for myself you could never prove by my references, verify by my employers, nor surmise by the way I sat the saddle, but I did for a brief span follow the cowboy calling. However, the West's most disparaging description for the inept, round-rumped rider "he couldn't ride in a covered wagon" could never apply to me. I still have the backside bunions—not to mention the thirty-six notches—to prove it. But as regards horses, that is something else. A big, gray, A. C. Hoover horse named (ironically) Reuben Roundass terminated my cowboy career when he stuck my head in the hard side of a hillside west of Ozona one hot August day of 1931. I came to my senses, to a certain extent, with a burning yearning for learning. Drawing the twenty-two dollars wages due me I applied it on a college degree—Sul Ross, 1935. Having been pampered, petted, and protected my last two years in high school, bedded and boarded free of charge by Grim and Molly Taylor—little did I dream that that twenty-two dollars would amount to approximately one third of the cash money I would require for four years of college. Sixty-seven dollars cash, to be exact, was what it took me to wind out the four years. On the side, however, there was considerable sanitary engineering, railroad boarding-house cooking, greenhouse gardening, housekeeping, pool parlor operating and summer cowboying, each dreary to the nth degree, except the latter.

For the last third of a hundred years I have had the pleasure of regrowing up with hundreds of school kids and a permanent school-marm partner, the guiding hand of whom has kept me settled and solvent lo these many years.